John Amos Comenius

John Amos Comenius

1592-1670

Selections

Introduction by Jean Piaget
*Director of the International Bureau
of Education*

*In commemoration of the
third centenary of the publication of
Opera Didactica Omnia
1657-1957*

Unesco

Published in 1957 by the United Nations
Educational, Scientific and Cultural Organization
19, avenue Kléber, Paris-16e
Printed by Imprimerie Centrale Lausanne S. A.

Foreword

At its ninth session, held in New Delhi during the months of November and December 1956, the General Conference of Unesco decided to publish a volume of excerpts from the works of J. A. Comenius, to celebrate the third centenary of the publication in Amsterdam of his *Opera Didactica Omnia*.

It was the desire of the General Conference that Unesco should be associated in the homage which educators throughout the world are paying to 'one of the first men to propagate the ideas which Unesco took for its guidance at the time of its establishment'.

Unesco is indebted to Professor Jean Piaget, director of the International Bureau of Education, for contributing the introduction to this work; to Professor Chlup, member of the Czechoslovak Academy of Science and president of the Comenius Institute of Prague, and to Mr. Patočka, lecturer at the University of Prague, for preparing the summaries and bibliography, as well as supplying valuable advice regarding the choice of texts; and to the Czechoslovak National Commission for Unesco for its aid and for making available the illustrations which appear in this volume.

Contents

Introduction

The significance of John Amos Comenius at the present time

Nothing is easier, or more dangerous, than to treat an author of three hundred years ago as modern and claim to find in him the origins of contemporary or recent trends of thought. A typical example of the difficulties this kind of interpretation meets with is the controversy about the significance of Francis Bacon's work (and the example is of particular interest here, since Bacon, as we know, was one of Comenius' sources of inspiration and was frequently quoted by him). Some authorities hold Bacon to be one of the precursors of modern experimental science; others find in his empiricism the whole residue of pre-scientific ways of thinking and emphasize how, as a theorist, he missed contact with the real science of his time, that of Galileo. Comenius could likewise be represented either as a precursor of evolutionary theory, genetic psychology, teaching methods based on child psychology, functional education and international education; or as a metaphysician who had no idea of the requirements of experimental psychological or even educational research, and who substituted the discussion of ideas for the analysis of facts. Yet all these extreme judgements would be incorrect.

The real problem is to find in Comenius' writings—our knowledge of which has been so much enriched by the discoveries of the group now working at the Comenius Institute in Prague—not what is comparable with modern trends, to the neglect of the rest, but what makes the vital unity of the thinking of the great Czech specialist in theory and practice; and to compare this with what we know and want today. Either Comenius can have no immediate interest for us at the present time or his interest for us depends on that central core of thought which is to be found in any system and which it should be possible to express in the form of a few simple ideas. In the first part of this introduction, we shall therefore try to discover the dominant ideas in Comenius'

thinking; then, in the two succeeding parts, we shall seek to bring out
the aspects of the great educationist's work which are still important for
us, in the light of these central ideas restated in terms accessible to us.

I

When we go through the mass of Comenius' writings, however, it is
extremely difficult to pick out the guiding ideas of the system, which is
full of obscurities, and sometimes of apparent contradictions.

In the first place, how are we to account for the fact that a theologian
enamoured of metaphysics and imbued with the speculative spirit of the
seventeenth century should have concerned himself with education to
the point of creating a 'Great Didactic'? There were indeed many
educational institutions in which certain special methods had been developed; and these had been described. Ratke and Alsted, for instance,
were probably the first to draw Comenius' attention to teaching problems, especially in the field of language instruction. But there was a long
way to go before building up a whole philosophy of education and cent-
ring a still broader system around it. Thinkers and philosophers, from
Montaigne and Rabelais to Descartes and Leibniz, had likewise made
profound remarks about education, but only as corollaries to their main
ideas. Not only was Comenius the first to conceive a full-scale science of
education but, let it be repeated, he made it the very core of a 'pansophy'
which, in his thinking, was to constitute a general philosophic system.
How can we explain so original and unusual a statement of problems,
in the middle of the seventeenth century?

The spirit in which Comenius sought to write the unfinished work
known as the 'General Consultation' was the best proof that the art of
teaching was intended to be the core of 'pansophy' itself; it also, incidentally, accounts for the failure of the enterprise. Instead of building up in
the abstract that total, indivisible body of knowledge, that universal
science that was to be pansophy—the doctrine of the progressive achieve-
ment of the 'world of ideas' within the superimposed worlds whose
parallel strata form the universe—Comenius was forced, because he was
pursuing a didactic as well as a philosophical aim (and this, by the way,
is the most interesting aspect of the work), to make simplifications and
assimilations which finally proved too much for him. He wished to
construct his own system, but he also cherished the ambition of providing a kind of introduction to philosophy for all. Such an undertaking

was unique in the seventeenth century. Hence the same problem: how are we to explain this merging of the need for a systematic basis for education with general philosophical speculation?

There is another difficulty. The foreword to *The Great Didactic* contrasts, with calm daring, the *a priori* method the author intends to follow, with the empirical or *a posteriori* teaching experiments characteristic of the educational work of his predecessors. 'We are so bold as to promise a *Great Didactic* ... a complete treatise on how to teach all subjects to all men, and how to teach them in such a way that the result will be certain. . . .' 'We shall show that all this is done *a priori*, that is to say, deriving from the immutable nature of things ... and that a universal system is thus established which is valid for the institution of universal schools.'[1] But this promise of an *a priori* science of education, an 'enormous' undertaking, as Comenius himself admits, seems to come to nothing when we seek the basis for this science teaching, for example, and find that Comenius is content with the theory of sensation: 'Truth and certitude of knowledge depend only upon the evidence of the senses', or 'The certainty of knowledge is proportionate to the extent to which it is derived from sensation.'[2] There often seems to be some contradiction between the general principles the author proclaims and the quasi-sensualistic empiricism of so many of his formulae. Here again, it must therefore be assumed that there is an original connexion between these somewhat irreconcilable statements, and that there is a synthesis linking man with nature so as to show why the educative process is the keystone of this philosophy.

But there is still more to the problem. Education, according to Comenius, is not merely the training of the child at school or in the home; it is a process affecting man's whole life and the countless social adjustments he must make. Society as a whole is considered by Comenius *sub specie educationis*. The great principles of peace and the international organization of education that make him a forerunner of so many modern institutions and trends of thought likewise stem, in his work, from this unique synthesis between nature and man which we have just suggested as the central element of his speculation and as the explanation of the mystery of an educationist's philosophy in an age when education was a matter either of techniques unsupported by theory or of general

1. *The Great Didactic*. Introduction.
2. ibid., Chap. xx, and pp. 79-87 of the present work.

observations without any attempt to constitute a science of teaching or education.

The key of these difficulties can be discovered only if we can find more complex basic concepts in Comenius' philosophy than those which are ordinarily taken as sufficient—concepts whose very pattern is such as to make it possible to restate the central ideas of the system in modern terms. This explains the twofold impression of outmoded form and up-to-date substance which one continually receives when reading the great educationist's works.

In this respect, Comenius' metaphysics lies between scholasticism as inspired by Aristotle and the mechanicalism of the seventeenth century. Everyone can see the kinship between his philosophy and Bacon's but, in respect of empiricism, this direct connexion should not be over-stressed; the main points to be kept in mind are the return to nature and the *instauratio magna*. The Aristotelian language used by Comenius is evident enough; but he constantly tends to replace the immobile hier-archy of forms by the concepts of advance and emergence and by the idea of parallelism or harmony among the various kingdoms. In other words, he often sounds a Neo-Platonic note, and Jan Patočka has quite rightly laid stress on this influence, and on that of Campanella.[1]

This approach to the question does away with some of the difficulties and sheds an unexpected light on the main outlines of the work. The central idea is probably that of nature as a creator of forms, which, being reflected in the human mind, thanks to the parallelism between man and nature, makes the ordering of the educative process automatic. The natural order is the true principle of teaching, but the sequence is dynamic, and the educator can carry out his task only if he remains a tool in nature's hands. Education is thus an integral part of the formative process to which all beings are subject and is only one aspect of that vast develop-ment. The descent or 'procession', in which the multiplication of beings consists, is matched by the upward motion at the level of human activity; and this upward motion, which will lead us to the Millenium, merges into one spontaneous development of nature and the educative process. Education is therefore not limited to the action of school and family but is part and parcel of general social life. Human society is an educative society: though this idea was not explicitly stated until the nineteenth century, Comenius' philosophy gave him a glimpse of it. Hence the

1. See Jan Patočka, 'Philosophical Basis for Comenian Pedagogy', in *Ceskoslovenska Akademie věd* (*Pedagogica*, No. 2), 1957, pp. 137-77, in particular, page 145.

disconcerting ambition of the 'pansophic' conception—'to teach all things to all men and from all points of view'—and the fundamental union between the educational ideal and the ideal of international organization.

We can thus gain an idea of how Comenius as a metaphysician, and Comenius at grips with the countless practical problems he encountered as a language teacher and organizer of schools, managed to achieve an inner unity, finding it in the elaboration of a philosophy based on education. Comenius' genius lay in grasping that education is one aspect of nature's formative machinery and so integrating the educative process into a system in which this process is indeed the essential axis.

We can see at the same time how the proclamation, at the beginning of *The Great Didactic*, of an *a priori* science of education can be reconciled with the apparent sensualism of so many passages in that work. Comenius was not a sensualist, though, as we shall see, he possibly failed to make sufficient use of the parallelism between the *ratio* and the *operatio*[1] to emphasize the active character of cognition. In his view, however, sensation creates knowledge in that it provides signals, as it were, that set off the spontaneous activity of the mind and link it up with the spontaneous activity that creates material things. Just as art imitates nature, according to the Aristotelian formula, so sensation (and this is a departure from the views of the peripatetics) makes it possible to re-establish the harmony between the active order of things, which teaches, and the spontaneity of the perceiving subject.

Finally, we can understand why Comenius became the apostle of international collaboration in education itself. No doubt the fratricidal struggles which constantly forced him into tragic exile and ruined his career both as theologian and as educator gave him reasons for his internationalist convictions, just as his experimental work as a teacher provided the starting-point for his thinking on education. But just as his thinking on that subject was integrated into a conception of the world where education proceeds from the formative action of nature, so his social and international ideas eventually became an integral part of his general doctrine of harmony and advance.

In short, Comenius' system is internally consistent; and the main constituent links of that coherence, though not immediately apparent, account for the major educational principles, applying to social and inter-

1. *The Great Didactic*, II. 17.

national as well as to scholastic affairs, which the master continually expounded. Comenius' significance for our time must therefore be sought by reference to the axes of his system; or, in other words, we must try to bring a modern point of view to bear upon the system as such, rather than upon mere individual aspects of it which, if isolated from their context, would give rise to arbitrary interpretations. Despite appearances, Comenius is really closer to us in his conception of man's development as part and parcel of that of nature than in most of the special theses he defends in his *Didactic*.

II

Except in a few cases, the real difference between Comenius and us is the difference which lies between seventeenth-century and twentieth-century ways of thinking. We no longer believe that metaphysics will enable us to understand the development of the child or of man in society, or the interaction between man and nature, to say nothing of the laws of nature. We have put a series of separate sciences in the place of simple speculation, and Comenius' central ideas must be transposed into the context of the present day with due regard to this fundamental change in method. Such a transposition is quite legitimate; in the history of the sciences, ideas have often been presented philosophically before being built up scientifically into a more elaborate structure or subjected to systematic scientific checking. Atomistic concepts, those of conservation, etc., may be cited among countless possible examples.

Notwithstanding this difference in method, Comenius may undoubtedly be considered as one of the precursors of the genetic idea in developmental psychology, and as the founder of a system of progressive instruction adjusted to the stage of development the pupil has reached.

With regard to the first of these two points, Comenius has been interpreted either as a proponent of the theory of innate faculties—mental development being attributed to a mere maturation of preformed structures—or as an empiricist who considers the mind as a receptacle gradually filled by knowledge derived from sensation. This dual interpretation is, in itself, indicative of the author's real position. Like all partisans of spontaneity and activity in the subject, he is accused sometimes of leaning towards preformism and sometimes of exaggerating the part played by experience. Comenius' concept of the parallelism of man and nature should be closely scrutinized in connexion with this particular point. Such parallelism is open to the two objections mentioned above

Portrait of J. A. Comenius, by Max Svabinsky.

if it is conceived as static, but it is a doctrine of dynamism to the extent that it links together the formative order of the material world and that formative order, inherent in the subject's actions, which, according to Comenius, represents both the law of development and the educative process itself.

With regard to the second point—application to teaching—Comenius works out all the implications of his belief in development. He distinguishes four types of schools for what we should now call the four major periods or stages in education: infancy, childhood, adolescence and youth. And, with really remarkable intuition, he grasps the fact that the same forms of knowledge are necessary at each of the different levels, because they correspond to permanent needs; and that the difference between these levels lies mainly in the way in which the forms of knowledge are re-outlined or restated. In a passage of *The Great Didactic* to which Mr. Piobetta rightly calls attention in the introduction to his French translation, Comenius presents the following proposition regarding these successive types of schools, which shows deep psychological understanding: 'Though these schools be different, we do not wish them to teach different things, but rather the same things in a different manner. I mean, all things which can make men truly men, and the learned truly learned; they should be taught in consideration of the pupil's age and the standard of his prior preparation, which should always tend gradually upward.' This is a very accurate anticipation of the successive reconstructions of the same kind of knowledge from stage to stage (e.g., from action to simple representation and thence to reflection), according to the system of consecutive development which modern genetic psychology has enabled us to analyse.

More generally, in the sixth of the 'Principles for Facilitating Teaching and Study', Comenius derives from the idea of spontaneous development the following three rules, which might be written in letters of gold on the door of every modern school—so applicable are they still, and unfortunately so seldom applied:

'Send children to school for as few hours as possible, I mean, four hours, and leave the same amount of time for individual study.

'Avoid overloading the memory; I mean, have only essential matters learnt by heart, leaving the rest to independent exercises.

'Base all teaching on the pupil's capacities as they are developed in the course of time and progress in school.'[1]

1. *The Great Didactic*, Chap. XVII.

In other words, if the child is really a being in process of spontaneous development, then individual study, independent exercises, and the transformation of capacities with age are possible; the school should therefore take advantage of such possibilities instead of ignoring them on the assumption that all education can be reduced to external, verbal and mnemonic transmission of adult knowledge through the teacher's words to the pupil's mind. True, in many other passages, Comenius seems to lay stress on receptivity. The role of images and sense data, the metaphor of the funnel into which knowledge is poured, and many other similar texts, appear to contradict these other statements. But if we bear in mind the idea of the parallel between formative nature and the training of man, it is impossible not to regard the above three rules as indicative of a recognition of the role of active development.

If we now go into the details of this theory of education based on spontaneous development, we are struck by the modern sound of a whole series of statements, despite the absence of a clear-cut theory of the relationship between action and thought.

To take this last point first, Comenius' general theory involves a concept of parallelism or corresponding harmony rather than dependence between the cognitive functions or organs (*mens, cerebrum, ratio*) and activities themselves (*manus, operatio, artes*). But as soon as he comes to deal with teaching, he corrects his approach and steadily affirms the primacy of action: 'Craftsmen do not hold their apprentices down to theories; they put them to work without delay so that they may learn to forge metal by forging, to carve by carving, to paint by painting, to leap by leaping. Therefore in schools let the pupils learn to write by writing, to speak by speaking, to sing by singing, to reason by reasoning, etc., so that schools may simply be workshops in which work is done eagerly. Thus, by good practice, all will feel at last the truth of the proverb: *fabricando fabricamur*.'[1]

Comenius goes as far as to defend this principle even in language teaching, stressing particularly that examples must precede rules: as the natural course of development consists in acting first and only afterwards reflecting on the circumstances of the action, examples cannot be deduced from a rule unless the rule is understood, but understanding of the rule derives from the retroactive organization of examples already utilized in spontaneous practice.[2]

1. Quoted from: P. Bovet, *J. Amos Comenius*, Geneva, 1943, p. 23.
2. *The Great Didactic*, Chap. XVI.

This principle of prior activity is interpreted by Comenius in the broadest sense, in accordance with his doctrine of spontaneity, as calling into play simultaneously needs and interests, or affective motivation, and functional practice as a source of knowledge. In other words, Comenius does not want exercises in a vacuum or mere breaking-in through action, but activity based on interest. P. Bovet, in this connexion, quotes several remarkable passages. The first among them are interesting for their broad scope: 'Do not undertake any teaching without first arousing the interest of the pupil' (XXX, II). And again: 'Always offer something which will be both agreeable and useful; the pupils' minds will thus be primed and they will come forward eagerly, with ever-ready attention.'[1] A third passage is interesting from the point of view of psychology. When a subject of teaching does not meet any clearly determined need, Comenius suggests recourse to the procedure of beginning something and then breaking off in order to create a gap—to start telling a tale or a little story, for instance, and break it off in the middle. What Comenius is using here, is not exactly a need, but what the psychologist K. Lewin, who has studied the effect of such interrupted action, has called 'quasi-needs'.

This functional character of the activity or spontaneity in which Comenius believes naturally leads him to take a clear stand with regard to the relationship between practical and formal methods. The question is discussed in an interesting way in connexion with the second principle of the 'Necessary Conditions for Teaching and Learning', which is expressed as follows: 'Nature prepares matter before giving it a form.' After a few reflections upon the need for school equipment (books, pictures, specimens, models, etc.) before lessons begin, Comenius takes up the central question of the relations between speech and the knowledge of things. As a former teacher of Latin and other languages he pronounces this decisive verdict: 'Schools teach how to prepare a speech before teaching the knowledge with which the speech should deal; for years, pupils are obliged to learn the rules of rhetoric; then, at some time, they are at last allowed to study the positive sciences, mathematics, physics, etc. And since things are substance and words accidents, the thing the grain and the word the straw, the thing the almond and the word the skin and shell, they ought to be presented to the human mind at the same time; *but* (and the underlining is mine) *care must be taken to start with things,* for they are the subject dealt with by the intellect as well

1. P. Bovet, loc. cit., pp. 18 and 24.

as by discourse.'[1] In other words, behind the Aristotelian language of matter and form, or substance and accident, Comenius reverts to the progressive sequence of structure building; and, as a teacher, he is fully aware of the harm done by that enduring curse of education—verbalism or pseudo-knowledge (*flatus vocis*) associated with mere words, as distinct from the real knowledge created by the action of the pupil upon the objects of his study. Generally speaking, the terms of the second of the 'Principles for Facilitating Teaching and Study' are still more eloquent than those of the other second principle just mentioned: 'Nature', says Comenius, 'predisposes matter to become desirous of form.'[2] From the educational point of view, this amounts to saying that functionally acquired knowledge ('in any event, young pupils must be imbued with the ardent desire to know and learn') tends spontaneously to become organized; it can therefore be co-ordinated with logical and verbal structures wherever such co-ordination is based upon a sound, 'form-desiring' initial content. Formal instruction that precedes understanding of the content, on the other hand, leads us back to verbalism.

Two of these 'Principles for Facilitating Teaching and Study' deserve special mention because they emphasize what we should now call the genetic aspect, and the functional aspect, of Comenius' ideas on educational psychology. Principle VII is stated as follows: 'Nature imparts stimulus only to fully developed beings who wish to break out of their shell.' Principle VIII: 'Nature helps itself in every possible way.' Comenius draws from these statements the following two corollaries which once again clearly assert the twofold need for education by degrees in accordance with the different stages of mental development and for a system of teaching that does not reverse the natural sequence of matter and form: 'Violence is done to the intellect (1) whenever the pupil is obliged to carry out a task which is beyond his age and capacities; (2) whenever he is bidden to learn by heart things which have not been clearly explained and understood.'[2]

But the statement which probably gives the clearest indication of the genetic trend in Comenius' ideas on education, is Principle I itself: 'Nature awaits the favourable moment.' After recalling that animals reproduce, and plants grow, according to the seasons, Comenius urges that the favourable moment for exercising the intelligence be seized upon, and that exercises 'all be performed gradually following a fixed

1. *The Great Didactic*, Chap. XVI.
2. Ibid., Chap. XVII.

rule'. This is again tantamount to stressing what, in modern parlance, would be called the sequence of stages of development.

We all know, however, how misleading such principles may be with regard to the actual practice of teaching. How many schools invoke the ideas of development, interest, spontaneous activity, etc., although, in real fact, the only development is that laid down in the curriculum, the only interests are imposed, and the only activities suggested by adult authority ! The true measure of active teaching (a form of education which is perhaps almost as rare today as in the seventeenth century) appears to be the way in which truth is established. There is no authentic activity so long as the pupil accepts the truth of an assertion merely because it is conveyed from an adult to a child, with all the aura of explicit or implicit authority attached to the teacher's words or those of the textbooks; but there is activity when the pupil rediscovers or reconstructs truth by means of external, or internal mental, action consisting in experiment or independent reasoning. This all-important fact appears to me to have been clearly grasped by Comenius. At the last school of which he was head, at Saros Patak in 1650, he was led to reduce his fundamental principles of teaching to three:[1]

1. Proceed by stages.
2. Examine everything oneself, without abdicating in the face of adult authority (what Comenius called, in the etymological sense of the word, 'autopsy').
3. Act on one's own impulsion: 'Autopraxy'. 'This requires that, with reference to all that is presented to the intellect, the memory, the tongue, and the hand, the pupils shall themselves seek, discover, discuss, do and repeat, without slacking, by their own efforts, the teachers being left merely with the task of seeing whether what is to be done is done, and done as it should be.'

Such an ideal of intellectual education is bound to go hand in hand with ideas on moral education, and these will serve as a kind of cross-check to verify to what extent Comenius has value for us today. In an age when the cane was a teaching instrument (it was still recommended by Locke !) and the only school morality was a morality of obedience, could Comenius, as we do today, extract from the concepts of development and spontaneous activity, a form of moral education which would also be an extension of those formative tendencies of nature to which the great

1. P. Bovet, loc. cit., pp. 34-5.

educationist constantly refers in the parallel he draws between nature and man ?

The touchstone in such a matter will be the question of retributive justice or punishment. And Comenius is radically opposed to corporal punishment: 'Beatings are of no use in inculcating a love of school work, but they are extremely likely to arouse aversion and hatred for it. Therefore, when it is seen that distaste for study threatens the pupil, the sickness must be cured, first by diet and then by gentle remedies; it must not be exacerbated by strong medicine. The sun itself offers us an excellent example of such prudence: it does not, in early spring, blaze suddenly upon new, tender plants to overwhelm them with the fire of its rays. . . . The gardener shows the same foresight, handling new plants skilfully and delicate shrubs with greater care. He spares them the wounds inflicted by pruning shears, knife and sickle. A musician, if his guitar, his harp or his violin be out of tune, does not strike the strings with his fist or with a stick. Nor does he rub the instrument against a wall, but puts forth all his skill to give it back its musical accents. In the same way, a harmonious love of study must be developed in the pupils, if we do not want their indifference to change into hostility and their apathy into stupidity.'[1]

But these decisive arguments against corporal punishment are not the only ones put forward by Comenius. His whole chapter on school discipline shows his effort to use positive sanctions (encouragement, emulation, etc.) rather than negative ones. In short, his disciplinary pedagogy shows the same spirit as his philosophy, where the theologian really gives little emphasis to original sin but speaks in constant praise of nature 'in perpetual progress' (cf. the title of Principle VII concerning the soundness of education and the school).

Besides these ideas on sanctions, Comenius' central concept of moral education is again a functional one, illustrating his preference for practice by experience as against compulsion or verbal instruction: 'One learns to be virtuous by accomplishing acts of virtue. By knowing we learn to know; by acting we learn to act. Since children easily learn to walk by walking, to speak by speaking, to write by writing, etc., they will also learn obedience by obeying, abstinence by abstaining, truth by being truthful, firmness by being firm, etc., provided always that there is someone to show them the way by precept and example.'[2]

1. *The Great Didactic*, Chap. XXVI.
2. Ibid., Chap. XXIII.

But he who shows the way is not necessarily an adult. In a curious passage of the *Methodus Linguarum Novissima* quoted by P. Bovet, Comenius lays stress on imitation and group games, bringing his systematic mind to outlining the seven characteristic factors of such games. He appears, in this connexion, to have recognized the role of the social relationship set up among players of games, as well as the role of competition and the rules imposed upon players by the game.

After emphasizing that these master concepts of Comenius' theory of education are still very up to date today, we must say a few words about his ideas on school organization. This topic will lead us, in the last part of our Introduction, to the social and international aspects of his doctrine.

At a time when education had neither stable institutions nor general programmes of study, Comenius endeavoured both to build up a rational administrative structure and to develop graduated, coherent programmes. All this elaborately detailed planning was dominated by a twofold requirement of unity: horizontal unity in respect of curricula at a given level, and vertical unity in the hierarchy of the stages of education.

In the first of these two respects, it is striking that Comenius, in the sphere of science teaching (which does not appear to have been his favourite speciality), has a very lively, very modern feeling of the interdependence of the sciences, necessitating co-ordination of the syllabuses: 'From all this (thoughts on the interaction of the parts of a system) it follows that the teaching of the sciences is bad when it is fragmentary and gives no general outline of the programme of study; no one can be perfectly instructed in a particular science unless he has some idea of the other sciences.'[1]

It is also interesting to see the importance Comenius attributes to the principle of the integration of previously acquired knowledge with that acquired later, following a pattern which is now matched even in our concepts of development.

As regards school organization, mention has already been made of the principle of subdivision into different levels corresponding to the various stages in mental development: the nursery school (or 'mother's knee') for infants; the public or national school for children; the grammar school or secondary school for older children; and academies for students. But another very interesting point about this organization is that Comenius wishes it to be the same for everyone—one school system for all: 'All young people of both sexes should be sent to public schools . . .

1. *The Great Didactic*, Chap. XVI.

All young people should first be sent to the national schools, even though some people, such as Zopper and Alsted, are of a contrary opinion and recommend that only boys and girls who will later engage in manual occupations should be sent to them. In their view, it is not to the elementary national school, but directly to the grammar school or gymnasium that young boys should be sent when their parents wish them to acquire deeper intellectual culture. My method of teaching, however, obliges me to take a different view.'[1]

But Comenius is not satisfied merely with these general principles. He expresses astonishingly prophetic views on a number of questions. Two examples may be given here.

One of them concerns the education of girls. In this regard, he insists upon complete equality of the sexes, in accordance with his pansophic principle that everything must be taught to everyone. 'No good reason can be advanced for depriving the weaker sex (let me give a personal opinion on this point) of the study of the sciences, whether they are taught in Latin or in a vernacular. In reality, women are endowed with a ready intelligence which makes them just as fitted as we are, and sometimes more so, for understanding the sciences. The way to high destiny is open to them, as it is to us. They are often called upon to govern States . . . to practise medicine and other arts of use to human kind. . . . Why should we merely let them learn their ABC and then lock them away from the study of books ?'[2]

But if these statements in favour of women's education are a logical consequence of his system (and that in no way diminishes Comenius' merit in remaining consistent), another corollary is much more surprising for the middle of the seventeenth century. It is his plea for the backward, 'the naturally weak and limited intelligences'. He states the 'urgent obligation to cultivate all minds. The weaker and more stupid a child is intellectually, the more help he needs to overcome his stupidity. . . . No mind can be so ill-endowed that it cannot gradually be improved by education.'[2]

We thus see how the architecture of a system in which a parallel is established between man and perpetually formative nature inspires not only a functional system of education, but also a conception of the general organization of education. This leads us on to the social and international aspects of the doctrine.

1. *The Great Didactic*, Chap. XXIX.
2. Ibid., Chap. IX.

III

An attempt has been made in the foregoing to show how up to date are Comenius' ideas on education and, in particular, how up to date is his methodology. The most surprising, and in many respects the most modern, aspect of his doctrine has been kept till the last—his ideas on education for everyone and for all peoples, and (what is still more astonishing) on the international organization of public education. This side of his work is what is most likely to interest Unesco, and in some respects Comenius may be regarded as one of that Organization's precursors.

The starting point of the sociological aspect of his educational philosophy is the statement of the universal right to education on a basis of equality. If we bear in mind Comenius' conception of society as an educative society, this is simply a direct corollary of his ideas on man's place in nature. But the corollary is an extremely bold one, when we consider this ideal of democratic education in its seventeenth-century historical context. 'If this universal instruction of youth be brought about by the proper means', says Comenius, 'none will lack the material for thinking and doing good things. All will know how their efforts and actions must be governed, to what limits they must keep, and how each must find his right place. . . . The children of the rich and the nobles, or those holding public office, are not alone born to such positions, and should not alone have access to schools, others being excluded as if there were nothing to be hoped from them. The spirit bloweth where and when it will.'[1]

In a word, the system of education proposed by Comenius is universal by its very nature; as he says, it is 'pansophic'. It is intended for all men, irrespective of social or economic position, religion, race or nationality. It must be extended to all peoples, however 'underdeveloped', as we say today, they may be; and Comenius would have commended the modern literacy campaigns undertaken for the purposes of fundamental education and social reintegration.

Comenius has sometimes been criticized for neglecting individuality. It would be easy to show that this is not the case; the importance he attributes to spontaneity, to interest, to the pupil's own ability to verify statements, and to 'autopraxy' would be meaningless if there were no respect for each child's individuality and the ways in which it differs from others. But he was mainly concerned about the universal application of his doctrine. In radical opposition to Jesuit education, which, at that

1. Quoted by J. Piobetta, *La Grande Didactique*, Presses Universitaires de France, Paris, 1952, p. 26.

time, was designed exclusively for those on the top rungs of the social ladder, Comenius defended his universalistic scheme and its intensely democratic implications, with his ideas of a single school system and the obligation of the upper classes to see to the education of a nation's entire youth. The democratic character of Comenius' reform is not his least title to fame; it explains why he is included among the great forerunners in Soviet education, as well in that of other countries.

But the 'pansophic' plan of teaching everything to everyone, and from every point of view, had many other implications, since, from the outset, it was intended to lead to a re-education of society, an *emendatio rerum humanarum*. To have a method is not enough: the means to apply it must also be found; that is, it must be introduced into a body of legislative provisions designed to ensure its propagation.

Nothing is more moving, in following Comenius' career, than the fact that this eternal exile, eternally a member of a minority group, never tired of drawing up plans for international collaboration: general schemes for universal peace, proposals for collaboration among the Churches, more specialized plans for international societies for erudite research, but, above all, plans for the international organization of public education and the final project for a *Collegium lucis*, which was to be a kind of international Ministry of Education (convincing evidence on this last point will be found in the collection of Comenius' writings contained in this volume).

But in order to understand these various points, we must very briefly outline Comenius' wandering life and his countless schemes that were thwarted by events. It would have been rather banal and academic to begin this introduction with a sketch of Comenius' life (with which everyone is familiar);[1] but it will be well to remind the reader of certain features of it in connexion with the study of his successive efforts and undertakings in the international field.

Born on 28 March 1592 at Uherský Brod in Moravia, he was left an orphan at an early age, and his guardians gave so little thought to his education that he was 16 before he could begin his Latin studies at the school of Prerov. His position as an orphan deprived of primary education no doubt did more to make him think about the relationship between school and personal work than a regular school upbringing would have done. With other young men belonging to the community of the Moravian

---

1. Comenius outlined the history of his own intellectual development several times, and modern historians have only slightly retouched the portrait he left of himself.

Brethren (the famous Protestant sect), he was later sent to the Academy of Herborn where he studied Protestant theology, attended Alsted's courses, and became familiar with Ratke's famous Memorial on language teaching. He soon began to write a book of the same kind for the Czech public, and also embarked on a Latin-Czech glossary which he continued to perfect over a period of 40 years. On his return to Moravia, he became a schoolmaster and later the church pastor at Fulnek; but the insurrection in Bohemia which originated the Thirty Years' War was the beginning of his misfortunes. He fled from his home, lost his wife and young children, and began to wander from one lordly domain to another, writing works of consolation for his co-religionists and preaching a resigned withdrawal into the inner life of the mind. Expelled from Bohemia, he took refuge at Leszno in Poland, where the Moravian Brethren had a centre and there, at the town's secondary school, resumed teaching. It was then that he developed his ideas on education, basing himself in particular on Bacon and Campanella, those 'happy restorers of philosophy'. And it was then, too, that he started to grapple with the great problem of his time, that of method. He wrote his *Janua Linguarum Reserata*, which was extremely successful, and his *Great Didactic* (originally written in Czech). But in his eyes these works were only stepping-stones to far more important objectives: he aimed at nothing less than a radical reform of human knowledge as well as of education. *The Great Didactic* itself was full of general ideas, but Comenius wished to unite and systematize them in a universal science or 'pansophy' (a term in fairly current use at that time).

This was the beginning of his international vocation, for such a systematization of knowledge, to his mind, was bound up with the co-ordination of universal currents of ideas. Starting from that moment, all his undertakings were accompanied by efforts at co-operation on a larger or smaller scale.

His first objective was the reconciliation of the Churches. Certain English friends, who were also interested in the movement for conciliation, sought to get him away from Leszno and brought his work to the attention of Louis de Geer, a Swedish philanthropist of Dutch origin; they then published Comenius' pansophic programme, without his knowledge, under the title of the *Prodromus Pansophiae* (a book which attracted the attention of Mersenne and of Descartes himself) and in 1641 invited him to London to help bring about an understanding between King and Parliament and to found a circle for pansophic collaboration.

These attempts failed; yet from them Comenius derived fresh ardour with which to pursue his schemes for reforming human society and learning in general. A choice was open to him between an invitation from Richelieu to found a pansophic college in France, and one from Louis de Geer to reform Swedish schools. He chose the second offer, hoping, no doubt, to obtain Swedish political support for the Bohemian refugees. On the way, he met Descartes at Endegeest, and Jungius and Tassius in Hamburg, and found difficulty in realizing that they hardly shared his views on the forming of an international circle for pansophic research. In Sweden he was well received by Court society, but his particular Protestant views were viewed with some doubt by Lutheran public opinion. He settled at Elbling in East Prussia (which was then Swedish territory) and wrote his *Novissima Linguarum Methodus*. But this work he regarded as of merely secondary importance, his great problem being, more and more, the reform of human affairs.

After taking part in the *Colloquium Charitativum* held at Thorn in 1645 with a view to reconciling the Churches, he fell into disgrace with the Swedes (he had foreseen that this would happen but had persisted in his course, which does credit to his character). He also escaped the lures of the Catholic party, which had thought to make use of him, and without having achieved any practical gains, but having acquitted himself with dignity in difficult circumstances, he resumed a scheme for a work on the universal reform of human society by the following means: (a) unification of learning and its spread by an improved school system under the supervision of a kind of international academy; (b) political co-ordination through international institutions aimed at maintaining peace; (c) reconciliation of the Churches in a tolerant form of Christianity. The title of the work, *General Consultation on the Reform of Human Affairs*, shows that his idea was to submit a programme to those taking part in the great negotiations which had aroused and disappointed so many hopes during the seventeenth century.

Promoted to the rank of Bishop of the Moravians, Comenius returned to Leszno. In 1650, however, he went to Saros Patak in Transylvania in the—again ill-starred—hope of founding a pansophic college. There he wrote the *Orbus Pictus*, the first illustrated textbook, which met with great success. In 1654 he returned to Leszno, which was burnt on 25 April 1656, during the Swedish invasion of Poland. In the disaster, Comenius lost his library and many of his manuscripts, including the Latin-Czech glossary on which he had been working since his youth.

After this new misfortune, he went with his family to stay with Laurenz de Geer (the son of his former patron) in Amsterdam. He refused a teaching post but consented to the publication of his complete didactic works. He still sought to complete his *General Consultation*, but had not yet been able to do so when he died at Naarden in the Netherlands in 1670.

One of the reasons why this last work was not completed was probably the fact that its philosophical and theological basis was in contradiction with the trends of the time, which were towards the development of individual sciences, particularly mathematical physics. The total, indivisible, knowledge Comenius dreamed of had already been outstripped by the new ideal of emergent modern science. But the main reason for the failure is probably the one given earlier: the conflict between the didactic need to write a philosophy for everyone and the desire to build up pansophy itself.

None the less, this unfinished work is perhaps the one which most clearly shows the deep philosophical, educational and social consistency of Comenius' thought. The then widespread Neo-Platonic idea of a 'procession' followed by a 'return' of things to their source takes on a new, and a concrete, significance in Comenius' system, because the return can occur only at the level of human activity, of that 'artificial world' which he had the considerable merit of interpreting as natural, that is, as participating in the formative mechanisms of nature itself.

Comenius' international projects therefore cannot be divorced from his educational ideas or from his philosophy as a whole. Peaceful international organization and the sort of international Ministry of Education that the *Collegium lucis* was intended to be are not merely the outcome of the dreams with which a man whose tragic life had always prevented him from carrying out his educational intentions consoled himself. As we have seen in running through the stages of his life, Comenius constantly sought, with direct relation to his 'pansophic' ideal, to lay the foundations for that co-operation which was at least as close to his heart as his ideal of teaching. He must therefore be regarded as a great forerunner of modern attempts at international collaboration in the field of education, science and culture. It was not incidentally or by accident that he conceived such ideas, fitting in fortuitously with certain modern achievements, but as a consequence of the general conception of his system, which fused nature, human activity and the educational process into a single whole. Unesco and the International Bureau of Education owe him the respect and gratitude which a great intellectual predecessor deserves.

As a conclusion to this introduction, let us consider in what sense we may say that Comenius has a significance for our time.

His modernity does not lie in his methods of demonstration, since he was not master of the science of his time and did not understand the reasons which were bringing his contemporaries to develop separate sciences distinct from philosophy. But, by a paradox which is extremely instructive from the standpoint of the history of science, this metaphysician with his dreams of a complete knowledge of all things contributed, when he wrote his *Great Didactic* and his specialized treatises, to the creation of a science of education and a theory of teaching, considered as independent disciplines. This may probably be said to be his main claim to glory, without, as we have seen, underrating his social and international action.

What accounts for the paradox and explains, in general, why Comenius is still so up to date despite his antiquated metaphysical apparatus, is the fact that, in all the matters he took up, he was able to give an extremely practical significance to the key concepts of his philosophy. His two central ideas were no doubt that of nature as a creator of forms and that of the parallelism between the activity of man and the activity of nature. It matters little therefore that he should have been content with global, partly mystical, ideas about nature's forms and those of human organization. By making a more scientific study of the evolution of living beings, child development and social structures, we can rediscover Comenius' great truths, simply enlarging Comenius' framework but not destroying it. Whatever the terms used to describe these facts, it is true that children develop according to natural laws; that education must take such development into account; that human societies also evolve according to certain laws; and that education is likewise dependent upon social structures. Comenius is thus among the authors who do not need to be corrected or, in reality, contradicted in order to bring them up to date, but merely to be translated and elaborated.

The normative principles set forth by Comenius—his central idea of democratic education and his other basic idea of the need for international organization (in all fields, but especially in education)—far from being weakened by such a transposition, emerge yet sounder and of more present application.

But the supreme merit of the great Czech educationist lies in the fact that he raised a series of new problems. Theories may pass away, but problems endure. They are ceaselessly renewed and diversified and ever retain their initial virtue of guiding and inspiring investigation. In this respect, even inadequate or inaccurate theories have often, in the history of science and technology, been of decisive importance, just because of the new problems they have raised.

From this point of view, it matters little whether the genetic conception of education propounded by Comenius, and his ideas on mental development, were drawn from Neo-Platonic theories about the 'return' of beings or derived from some other philosophical source. The important thing is that, by placing this reascension at the level of human activity and in parallel with the formative processes of nature, he created a series of new problems for his century: mental development, the psychological basis of teaching methods, the relationship between school and society, the need to organize or regulate syllabuses and the administrative organization of education, and lastly, the international organization of research and education. To have realized that such problems exist and to have lost no opportunity of drawing attention to their vital importance for the future of mankind is the greatest claim to fame of the celebrated educationist in honour of whom Unesco is publishing the commemorative work for which I have had the honour of writing this introduction.

J. Piaget

REBUS OMNIA SPONTE FLUANT ABSIT VIOLENTIA

Motto of J. A. Comenius, illustrated by Crispin de Pas.

Selections

The manuals of Comenius achieved a great success, beginning already in the seventeenth century, and the pedagogical reforms which he had recommended penetrated into school methods. In the nineteenth century the study of the life and works of Comenius was developed, and the list of his known works grew considerably. Documents of prime importance were discovered thanks to the efforts of numerous scholars, among whom Jan Kvacala should be mentioned, and it was these discoveries which inspired the rise of research on Comenius. Many problems concerning his works remained to be solved; these problems bore upon the evolution of his philosophical and theoretical ideas and on the very existence of the great work announced under the title of Universal Consultation.

Today we possess new information on all these points. In 1931, Professor S. Soucek, of the University of Brno, announced the discovery in Leningrad of six manuscripts written during the last years of Comenius' life, the period during which most of his great pedagogical concepts were expounded. Among these works is a treatise of the greatest interest on metaphysics. In 1933, Mr. G. H. Turnbull, professor at the University of Sheffield, discovered in London the papers of Samuel Hartlib, for many years the friend and correspondent of Comenius. These documents include a large number of unpublished letters and the manuscripts of previously unknown works. On the basis of this discovery, Mr. Turnbull published a volume dedicated to Comenius and edited the unpublished works of the great educator. (Two Pansophic Works, 1951.) With the help of Professor Turnbull's discoveries we are now able to follow much more closely the evolution of Comenius' ideas.

In 1934, Mr. Cyzevsky, a philosopher and Slavic scholar, discovered during the course of his research in the orphans' home in Halle a manuscript consisting of the five parts of the Consultation which had been lost at the beginning of the eighteenth century. The manuscript had been partly drafted by disciples of Comenius, but it is simple to distinguish their contribution from that which can be incontestably ascribed to the hand of the master. Mr. Cyzevsky also discovered

35

other texts which had been printed during Comenius' lifetime. These recent dis-coveries permit us to view Comenius in a new light, that of a social reformer who, through education, seeks to unite mankind.

In the present volume we have endeavoured to present the texts which illustrate certain aspects of the pedagogy of Comenius as it is traditionally known (The Labyrinth, The Great Didactic). *It has seemed indispensable, however, to present also a number of excerpts from* The Pampaedia *and* The Panorthosia *which form a part of the* Consultation *rediscovered at Halle 20 years ago. Comenius holds up as his goal the participation of all men in a universal civilization.*

The Labyrinth of the World and the Paradise of the Heart

Comenius wrote this book in Czech in 1623, after the Battle of the White Mountain, which confirmed the triumph of the House of Austria and the Counter-Reformation party throughout the lands of the Bohemian crown (Bohemia, Moravia, Silesia and Lusatia). As a Protestant preacher, he was proscribed and lived in hiding for another ten years in remote districts of Bohemia, before leaving his country for ever. The 'labyrinth' image portrays a profoundly disrupted social system, and the allegory related in the book is a criticism of human society as Comenius saw it. A pilgrim who wishes to visit the world in order to choose his vocation views all the ranks and occupations of mankind, and finds shams and confusion reigning everywhere. He witnesses an attempt at reform by Solomon which ends in the discomfiture of the just. Finally, he withdraws from the world into his inner self and, as a true Christian finds solace in converse with Jesus Christ. Jesus reveals to him a society constituted by his true disciples whose lives are governed by the precept of disinterested love for one's fellow man. *The Labyrinth,* in some of its aspects, is related to certain ideas of Pascal; various details, moreover, resemble those found in Bunyan's *Pilgrim's Progress* and in the social utopias of Campanella, Andrea and other authors of the period. This book gives us a better understanding of Comenius' efforts to reform society, as it is here described by means of education.

The passages given in the present volume have been taken from the first part (*The Labyrinth of the World*). They include the introduction, which gives the key to the allegory, and the chapters on the position of scholars, magistrates and soldiers.

Chapter I

On the reasons for the Pilgrimage through the World

When I had attained the age when human intelligence begins to distinguish between good and evil, and saw the various ranks, orders, occupations, callings and endeavours at which men busy themselves, it appeared to me highly desirable to consider well which group of people to join and with what matters I should occupy my life.

2. Thinking much and often on this matter and weighing it diligently in my mind, I came to the decision that such a fashion of life as contained the least of care, turmoil and labour, but the greatest degree of comfort, peace and cheerfulness pleased me most.

3. But then again I found it difficult to discern which and what vocation that might be; and I knew not of whom to seek proper counsel; nor did I greatly wish to consult anyone on this matter, thinking that everyone would praise to me his own walk in life. Neither did I dare to grasp anything hastily for I feared that I might not choose aright.

4. Yet, I confess, I secretly began to grasp at now one thing, then another, then a third, but each one I speedily abandoned for I perceived (as it seemed to me) something of hardship and vanity in each. Meanwhile I feared that my fickleness would bring me to shame. And I knew not what to do.

5. After much inward struggle and turning the matter over in my mind I came to the decision that I should first look into all human affairs under the sun and then only, having wisely compared one with another, choose a vocation and arrange for myself the things necessary for leading a peaceful life in the world. The longer I thought of this plan, the better I liked it.

Chapter II

The Pilgrim obtains Ubiquitous as his Guide

Thereupon I came out of myself and began to look round thinking how and whence to begin. At that very instant, I knew not whence, there appeared a man brisk of gait, alert of glance, quick of speech, a man in fact whose feet, eyes, tongue, all seemed to me forever in motion. He stepped up to me, and asked whence I came and whither I was going. I answered that I had left my home and intended to wander about the world and gain some experience.

2. This pleased him well and he said: 'But where is thy guide?' I answered, 'I have none. I trust to God and to my eyes not to lead me astray.' 'Thou wilt not succeed', said he. 'Hast thou heard of the labyrinth of Crete?' 'I have heard somewhat', I answered. He then replied, 'It was a wonder of the world, a building consisting of so many chambers, closets, and corridors that he who entered without a guide walked and blundered through it in every direction and never found his way out. But that was mere child's play compared to the way in which the labyrinth of this world is fashioned, particularly in our own day. I, a man of experience, do not counsel thee to enter it alone.'

3. 'But where, then, shall I seek such a guide?' I asked. He answered, 'It is my task to guide those who wish to see and learn something and to show them where everything is. Therefore, indeed, did I come to meet thee.' Wondering, I said, 'Who art thou, my friend?' He answered, 'My name is Searchall, surnamed Ubiquitous. I wander through the whole world, peep into all corners, inquire about the words and deeds of all men; I perceive all that is to be seen, spy out and discover all that is secret; in short, nothing can befall unbeknownst to me; it is my duty to survey everything; and if thou comest with me, I shall lead thee to many secret places whereto thou wouldst never have found thy way.'

4. Hearing such speech I began to rejoice in my mind at having found such a guide, and begged him not to shun the labour of conducting me

through the world. He answered, 'As I have gladly served others in this matter, so I will gladly serve thee.' And seizing my hand, 'Let us go', he said. And we went. And I said, 'Well, now will I gladly see what the ways of the world are, and also whether it contains that on which a man may safely rely.' Hearing this, my companion stopped and said, 'Friend, if thou art starting on this voyage with the purpose, not of seeing our things with pleasure, but of passing judgement on them according to thine own understanding, I do not know how pleased Her Majesty, our Queen, will be with this.'

5. 'And who, then, is your Queen?' I said. He answered, 'She who directs the whole world and its ways from one end to the other. She is called Wisdom, although some wiseacres call her Vanity. Let me tell thee beforehand; when we go about and study things, do not be too wise, or else thou wilt bring hardship upon thyself and I may come in for my share with thee.'

Chapter III

Delusion joins them

Thus while he was talking with me, behold someone approached us. I could not tell whether it was a man or a woman (for he was wondrously muffled up and surrounded as it seemed in mist). 'Ubiquitous', he said, 'whither dost thou hurry with this man?' 'I am leading him into the world', he replied, 'for he wishes to behold it.'

2. 'And why without me?' the other again said. 'Thou knowest that it is thy duty to guide, mine to show where things are. For it is not the wish of Her Majesty the Queen that anyone who enters her realm should

interpret for himself what he sees and hears according to his pleasure, or be too wise about it; for he should be told the nature and purpose of the different things and should remain content therewith.'

Ubiquitous answered, 'Is there anyone so insolent as not to remain content with our order just as all others do ? But this one methinks will require a bridle. So, let us go forward !' Then he joined us, and we went on.

3. But I thought in my mind, 'I hope to God I shall not be misled. These fellows conspire to put some bridle upon me.' And I said to this, my new companion, 'Friend, take it not amiss; gladly would I know thy name also.' He answered, 'I am the interpreter of Wisdom, the Queen of the world, charged with the duty of instructing men how they can understand the things of the world, old and young, high-born and base-born, ignorant and learned, all that belongs to true worldly wisdom, and I lead them to joy and contentment; for without me even kings, princes, nobles and the proudest men would be in a strange despondency and would spend their time on earth mournfully.'

4. On this I said, 'Fortunately has God granted me thee as a guide, dear friend, if this is true. For I have set out for the world for the purpose of seeking what is safest and most gratifying in it so that I may lay hold of it. Having now in thee so trusty a councillor, I shall easily be able to choose well.' 'Have no doubt of it', he said, 'for though in our kingdom thou wilt find everything excellently and properly ordered and gay, and will perceive that all the Queen's loyal subjects do not fail to live comfortably, yet it is even true that some occupations and trades excel others in comfort and leisure. Thou wilt be able to choose from among them all. I will explain to thee everything as it is.' I said, 'By what name do men call thee ?' He answered, 'My name is Delusion.'

Chapter IV

The Pilgrim receives Bridle and Spectacles

Hearing this, I was terrified, and bethought myself what companions I had acquired for my sins. The first one (thus my mind devised) spoke of some sort of bridle; the other was called Delusion; his Queen he called Vanity (although he seemed to have let this slip out accidentally; but what was this?)

2. And whilst I thus continued silently and with downcast eyes and unwilling halting steps, Searchall says, 'What, thou fickle one, I suspect thou wishest to go back!' And before I could answer he threw a bridle over my neck, and the bit slipped suddenly into my mouth. 'Now wilt thou', he said, 'go more readily to where thou hast started for?'

3. I looked at this bridle and saw that it was stitched together of straps of shallowness, and the bit was made of the iron of pigheadedness, and I understood that I should now no longer journey through the world of my own free will, but that I should be forcibly driven by inconsistency and my thirst for knowledge.

4. Then my companion on the other side said, 'And I give thee these spectacles through which thou wilt henceforth look on the world.' And he thrust on my nose spectacles through which I saw immediately everything differently than before. They certainly had this power (as I tested it many times afterwards) that to him who saw through them distant things appeared near, near things distant, small things large, and large things small, ugly things beautiful, and beautiful things ugly; the white black, and the black white, and so on. I well understood that he should be called Delusion who knew how to fashion such spectacles and place them on men.

5. Now these spectacles, as I afterwards understood, were fashioned out of the glass of Illusion, and the rims which they were set in were of that horn which is named Custom.

6. Fortunately he had placed them on me somewhat crookedly so that they did not press closely on my eyes, and by raising my head and looking under them I was still able to see things clearly in their natural way. I rejoiced over this, and thought to myself, 'Though you have closed my mouth and covered my eyes, yet I trust in my God that you will not take from me my mind and my reason. I will go on and see what then this world is which the Lady Vanity wishes us to see, but not to see with our own eyes.'

Chapter X

The Pilgrim regards the Men of Learning; at first generally

And my guide said unto me, 'Now I understand where thy mind inclines. Among the learned men with thee. Life among the learned will have a lure for thee! It is an easier, quieter, and for the mind more useful life.' 'Yes, that is true', said the interpreter; 'for what could be more delightful than to abandon and no longer heed the struggles of this material life, and to employ oneself in studying these manifold beautiful things? Verily it is this that makes mortal men like unto the immortal God, and almost equal to him, when they become almost omniscient, knowing everything that is in heaven, on earth, or in the depths, or was or will be, although not everyone, it is true, receives these gifts in equal perfection.' 'Lead me there!' I said, 'Why dost thou tarry?'

2. And we arrived at a gate which they called 'Disciplina', and this was long, narrow, and dark, full of armed guards to whom everyone who entered the street of the Learned was to report, and to ask of them a safe conduct. And I saw how crowds of people, mainly young ones, came up and immediately underwent divers severe examinations. Each

one was first examined as to what pouch, what posteriors, what head, what brain (which they judged by the slime from the nostrils) and what skin he had. If, then, the head was of steel, the brain in it of quicksilver, the posteriors leaden, the skin iron, and the pouch golden, these men were praised and willingly conducted farther, but if one did not possess these five things, they ordered him back or, though foreboding ill success for him, haphazardly admitted him. And wondering at this, I said, 'Do they lay such stress then on these five metals that they search for them so industriously?' 'Very much indeed', said the interpreter; 'If one has not a head of steel it will burst; if he has not in it a brain of liquid quick-silver, he will not obtain in it a mirror; if he has not a skin of tin he will not endure the process of education; if he has not leaden posteriors, he will hatch nothing, miscarry all; and without a golden pouch, where will he obtain leisure, where masters, both living and dead? Or dost thou think that those things may be obtained without cost?' And I understood the drift of his words, that for the state of being learned, health, talent, perseverance, patience and money are necessary, and said, 'Truly can it therefore be said: *Non cuivis contigit adire Conrinthum*' [Not all wood is for seasoning].

3. And we passed on through the gate, and I saw that each guard, taking one or more of these men, led them on; then he blew something into their ears, wiped their eyes, cleansed their noses and nostrils, pulled out and clipped their tongues, folded and then disjoined their hand and fingers, and I know not what else he did not. Some even attempted to pierce the men's heads and pour something into them. My interpreter, seeing me afraid, said, 'Wonder not; learned men must have their hands, tongues, eyes, ears, brains and all internal and external senses different from the ignorant herd of men; therefore must they be here transformed, and without trouble and offence this cannot be.' Then I looked and beheld how dearly those poor wretches had to pay for their transforma-tion. I speak not of their pouches, but of their skins, which they had to expose; for fists, canes, sticks, birch rods struck them on their cheeks, heads, backs, and posteriors till they shed blood and were almost entirely covered with stripes, scars, bruises, and weals. Some, seeing this, before they surrendered themselves, cast a hasty glance inside the gate and ran away; others tore themselves out of the hands of the transformers and also fled. A smaller number only remained, until they were allowed to return into the open air; and feeling a desire for this profession, I under-went the formation though not without hardship and anguish.

4. When we passed through the gate, I saw that to each whose wit had thus been sharpened they gave a badge by which it could be known that he belonged among the learned men: an inkhorn at the girdle, a pen behind the ear, and in the hand an empty book for the purpose of seeking knowledge. I, too, received these articles. Then Searchall said to me, 'Now, here we have a fourfold crossways: to philosophy, medicine, jurisprudence, and theology; where shall we go first?' 'Do as you judge best', quoth I. To this he replied, 'Let us first go into the market-place where they all are; there canst thou behold them altogether; then will we proceed through the various lecture rooms.'

5. Thereupon he led me into the market-place where I beheld crowds of students, masters, doctors, priests, both youths and greybeards. Some of them were gathered in groups conversing and disputing; others betook themselves to corners, out of sight of the rest. Some of them (as I clearly perceived, but I dared not speak of it there) had eyes, but had no tongues; others had a tongue, but had not eyes; others had only ears, but neither eyes nor tongues; and so forth. Thus did I understand that shortcomings persisted even among them. But as I now saw that all those men came from a place and went back to it as bees swarm into and out of a beehive, I begged that we should go there too.

6. Thus we entered and there was a hall so large that I could not see its ending, and on all sides it was so full of many shelves, compartments, receptacles and vessels that a hundred thousand carts could not have removed them; and each one had its own inscription and title. And I said, 'What apothecary's shop have we entered?' 'Into an apothecary's shop', said the interpreter, 'where remedies against the ailments of the mind are kept; and this, by its proper name, is called a library. See what endless storehouses of wisdom are here!' Then looking round, I saw long rows of learned men, who arrived from all directions and turned round these things. Some chose the finest and most subtle among them, extracted morsels from them, and received them into their bodies, gently chewing and digesting them. Approaching one of them, I asked him what he was doing. He answered, 'I am getting on well.' 'And what taste is there in this', quoth I. And he again, 'As long as a man chews it in the mouth, he tastes bitterness and sourness, but afterwards it changes into sweetness.' 'And wherefore is this?' I said. He answered, 'It is easier for me to carry this within me and I am thus surer. Dost thou not see the use?' I looked at him with more care, and I saw that he was stout and fat, and of comely colour, his eyes glittered like candles, his speech was

careful and everything about him was lively. Then my interpreter said, 'Look at these.'

7. And I looked and saw some who bore themselves most greedily, cramming down everything that came into their hands. Then looking at them more carefully, I saw that their colour, their body and their fat had by no means increased save that their bellies only were swollen and puffed out. And I also saw that what they had crammed down again crept out of them undigested either above or below. Some of them even fainted or even lost their minds; others became pale, pined away, and even died. Seeing this, others pointed at them and told each other how dangerous it was to deal with books (for thus they called the vessels); some fled, others exhorted each other to handle them carefully. These therefore did not absorb everything; rather did they burden themselves in front and behind with bags and pouches into which they crammed the vessels (mostly those on which they saw written: Vocabulary, Dictionary, Lexicon, Promptuarium, Florilegium, Loci communes, Postillae, Concordancy, Herbaria, etc. according to what they deemed most fitting for their needs); these they carried with them and when they had to speak or write something they took from their pouches whatever was needed for their mouths or pens. Noting this, I said, 'These then carry their knowledge in their pockets?' The interpreter answered, 'These are Memoriae subsidia; hast thou not heard of them?' I had indeed heard this custom praised by some; they said that those who used it brought forth only learned things. And it may be thus, but I noted other incommodities. It befell in my presence that some had lost their vessels, while others, having laid them aside, had been deprived of them by fire. What a running about, wringing of hands, lamenting, and crying for help! For a time nobody wanted to dispute, write, or preach any longer; they walked along drooping their heads, cowering and blushing, and begged or purchased wherever they could another little outfit. Those, however, who had a store within them were not afraid of such a mishap.

8. Meanwhile, I saw others again who did not put these vessels into their pouches, but carried them into a closet; entering behind them I saw that they fitted out beautiful cases for them, painted them in various colours, sometimes even bordered them with silver and gold, placed them in shelves, and then drew them out again to look at them; then they did them up and again undid them, and walking to and fro, showed one another as well as other people how beautiful these things were—all this of course superficially; some also at times looked at the titles so that they

might be able to name them. 'What are these people playing at?' I asked. 'My dear comrade', the interpreter answered, 'it is a fine thing to have a fine library.' 'Even if you use it not?' said I. He answered, 'Those also who love their libraries are counted among the learned.' I thought within myself, 'Just as those who own a large number of hammers and tongs, but know not how to use them are counted among the blacksmiths.' But I dare not say this for fear of drawing something down on myself.

9. Then entering the hall again I saw that the number of the receptacles ever increased in every direction, and I watched to see whence they brought them, and saw that they were brought from behind a screen; going also behind it I saw many turners who—one more diligently and neatly than the other—were fashioning these vessels out of wood, bone, stone, and other materials; then filled them with salve or theriac, and delivered them up for general use. And the interpreter said to me, 'These are the men worthy of praise and all honour who serve their race with things most useful, who begrudge no labour, no endeavours to increase wisdom and learning, and who share their glorious gifts with others.' And the wish befell me to examine out of what stuff and in what manner these things (which he called gifts and wisdom) were made and prepared. And I observed one or two who collected fragrant roots and herbs, cut them up, crumbled them, boiled them and distilled them, preparing delightful theriacs, brews, syrups and other medicines which are useful to the life of man. On the other hand I saw some who only picked out things from the vessels of others and transferred them into their own; and of these there were hundreds. And I said, 'These merely pour on water.' The interpreter answered, 'Even thus learning is increased; for cannot one and the same thing be done now in this, now in that fashion? Moreover, something can always be added to the first elements, and they can thus be improved.' 'And spoilt also', I said with anger, seeing plainly that fraud was being practised here. Some also, seizing the vessels of others, filled up several of their own, and diluted the contents as much as they could, even pouring in slops; another condensated the mixture by adding every sort of hodge-podge, even dust and sweepings only that it might appear to be freshly made up. Then they labelled them with titles even more pompous than those of the others, and impudently, like other quacks, extolled their own wares. Then I both wondered and angered that (as I said before) hardly ever did anyone examine the internal substance; rather did they seize indiscriminately whatever came first. And if some did choose they were guided only

47

by the outward appearance and the inscription. And I then understood why so few attained the inward freshness of the mind, for the more of these medicines each man devoured, the more he vomited, turned pale, faded and decayed. And I saw also that a large number of these delightful medicaments were not even used by men, but left to the moths, worms, spiders and flies, to dust and mould, to some dark press or remote corner. Fearing this fate, some, as soon as they had completed their theriac (some even before they had begin it in earnest) ran to their neighbours asking them for prefaces, verses, anagrams; then they searched for patrons who should lend their names and purses to the new compounds; then wrote the titles and inscriptions in the most ornate fashion; then embellished the divers figures and engravings with curling flowers; also they themselves carried them among the people, pressed and, so to speak, even thrust the goods upon them. But I saw that even this availed not in the end because of the over-accumulation of the stuff. And I pitied some who, although they could have enjoyed simple quiet, yet gave themselves to this quackery without any necessity or use, and, indeed, at the risk of their good name, and to the harm of their neighbours. But when I gave news of this I earned but hatred as if I had injured the common welfare. I am silent as to how some prepared these their concoctions out of materials that were plainly poisonous so that as many poisons as medicaments were sold, and unwillingly did I bear such evil, but there was no one to set it right.

10. Then we returned to the market-place of the Learned and behold, there were quarrels, strife, scuffles, tumult among them. Rarely was there one who had no contention with another; for not only the young ones (with whom it could be imputed to the insolence of undeveloped youth), but even the old men were stealing from one another. For the more learned one considered himself or was so considered by others, the more quarrels he began and the more he attacked his neighbours with fencing, slashing, hurling and shooting till it was fearful to behold; and he founded his honour and glory on this. And I said, 'But in the name of dear God what is this? I had thought, and this was I promised, that this was the most peaceful of occupations.' The interpreter answered, 'My son, thou dost not understand this; these men only sharpen their wits.' 'What! Thou sayest they sharpen their wits! But I see wounds, and blood, and wrath, and murderous hatred of the one against the other. The like of this I have not even witnessed among the craftsmen.' 'No doubt', he said, 'for the arts of such men are but handicrafts, slavish arts,

while those of these others are the liberal arts. Therefore what is not allowed nor would be tolerated to them, the others have full liberty to do.' 'But how this can be called order', I said, 'I know not.' It is true that apparently their arms did not seem terrible. For the spears, swords, and daggers with which they hacked and stabbed one another were of leather, and they held them not in the hand, but in the mouth. Their firearms consisted of reeds and quills, which they loaded with powder that had been dissolved in water, and then they threw sheets of paper at each other. Nothing of this, say I, viewed superficially, appeared terrible; but when I saw that if a man was even slightly struck, he jerked, screamed, reeled, fled, I easily understood that this was no jesting but a real fight. Sometimes many pressed one hard, till everywhere around the noise of swords danged in the ears, and paper bullets fell on him like hail; sometimes a man, defending himself bravely, succeeded in dispersing all his assailants; another succumbed to the blows, and fell. And I beheld here cruelty, quite unusual elsewhere, for they spared neither the wounded nor the dead, but they hacked and stabbed all the more unmercifully him who could no longer defend himself, mostly endeavouring to show their valour in this fashion. Some dealt with each other in a more moderate manner, but even these were not free from disputes and misunderstandings. For as soon as anyone uttered a word, instantly another stood up to oppose him so that they even wrangled as to whether snow was white or black, fire hot or cold.

11. Meanwhile some interfered in these disputes and began to counsel peace; of this I was glad. A rumour arose that all disputes would be settled; and the question arose who was to accomplish this? The answer was that by permission of Queen Wisdom the most judicious from all estates should be chosen and power given unto them—after hearing the adverse parties—to discriminate among the divers opinions with regard to all things and to pronounce which was the truer opinion. And many crowded together who either were to be or wished to be judges; there assembled, in particular, a large number of those who had had dissensions because of the differences of their views. Among these I saw Aristotle with Plato, Cicero with Sallust, Scotus with Aquinas, Bartolus with Baldus, Erasmus with the men of the Sorbonne, Ramus and Campanella with the Peripatetics, Copernicus with Ptolemy, Theophrastus with Galen, Hus, Luther, and others with the Pope and the Jesuits, Brenz with Beza, Bodin with Wier, Sleidan with Surius, Schmiedlein with the Calvinists, Gomarus with Arminius, the Rosicrucians with

4

philosophasters, and countless others. When the arbiters ordered them to bring forward their accusations and complaints, proofs and inferences in the briefest possible written form, they laid down such piles of books that six thousand years would not have been sufficient to examine them; and they asked that this summary of their propositions should for the time be accepted, but that each one should have full liberty, later, when the necessity showed itself to more fully explain and expound his views. And they began to look at these books, and as soon as a man began to look at one of them, he became intoxicated and began to defend it. Thus there arose among the arbiters and mediators a great dissension when one man defended one view, another some other. And having thus settled nothing, they dispersed, and the learned men again returned to their squabbles. This grieved me to tears.

Chapter XIX

The Pilgrim regards those Invested with Authority

We then entered another street where I saw on all sides a countless number of chairs, some higher and some lower; they called those who sat on them His Worship the Sheriff, His Worship the Mayor, The Worshipful Magistrate, His Lordship the Regent, His Lordship the Burgrave, His Lordship the Chancellor, His Excellency the Governor, Their Lordships the Lords Justices, Gracious King, Prince, Lord, and so forth. And the interpreter said to me, 'Now thou hast before thee the men who deliver judgements and sentences in lawsuits, punish evil-doers, defend the good, and maintain order in the world.' 'This is, indeed, a fine thing, and one that is necessary for mankind', I said; 'But whence do they take these men ?' He answered, 'Some are born to their office, some are elected to it either by these men or by the community, being deemed the wisest and the most experienced of all and the best versed in justice and law.' 'This is also fine', said I.

2. But at that moment I suddenly saw clearly, and I beheld that some obtained their seats by purchase, others by entreaty, others by flattery, while others, again, occupied them arbitrarily. Seeing this, I cried, 'Look, look what an abuse !' 'Hush, you meddler', said the interpreter, 'thou wilt fare ill if they hear thee !' 'And why do they not wait', said I, 'till they are chosen ?' He answered, 'What of it ! These men feel no doubt confident that they are capable of such work; if others accept them as such, what concern is that of thine ?'

3. So I kept silent, and after fixing my spectacles, I looked at these men attentively and witnessed an astounding sight: to wit, that hardly one of them possessed all his limbs; almost everyone of them was devoid of some necessary thing. Some had no ears through which they could hear the complaints of the subjects; some had not eyes to see the disorders around them; some had no nose to scent the unlawful plots of knaves; some had not a tongue to speak in favour of the dumb, oppressed ones; some had no hands with which to carry out the pronouncements of justice; many also had not a heart to do what justice requires.

4. But those who had all these things appeared to me to be woeful people; for they were continually importuned, so that they could neither eat nor sleep quietly, while the others spent more than half their time in idleness. And I said, 'Why then do they entrust law and justice to such men who lack the members necessary for the purpose ?' The interpreter answered that this was not so, but that it only appeared so to me, for he said, 'Qui nescit simulare, nescit regnare. He who would rule others must often not see, not hear, not understand, even if he sees, hears, understands. This, as thou art inexperienced in politics, thou canst not understand.' 'Yet on my faith', quoth I, 'I see they have nought of what they should have.' 'And I', said he, 'advise thee to be silent; otherwise I promise thee if thou ceasest not to be so wise, thou shalt find thyself in a place that will please thee not. Knowest thou not that censuring judges endangers the neck ?' Then I was silent and gazed quietly at everything. But it does not seem to me fitting that I should narrate all I saw in regard to each of the chairs. On two things only will I touch.

5. I observed most carefully the law-court of the senators, and I saw the names of the lords-justices were as follows: Judge Nogod, Judge

Lovestrife, Judge Hearsay, Judge Partial, Judge Loveself, Judge Love-gold, Judge Takegift, Judge Ignorant, Judge Knowlittle, Judge Dila-tory, Judge Hasty, Judge Dontcare; the president of them all and the supreme justice and primate was Lord Thus-I-Will-It. From their names I immediately began to perceive what manner of judges they were; but an example of it befell in my presence. Simplicity was accused by Spiteful of having defamed some good people by calling usurers misers, drunk-ards gluttons, and I know not what else. The witnesses were Calumny, Lie and Suspicion. As counsels Flattery appeared for one side, and Prattler for the other; but Simplicity declared that she needed him not. Question-ed whether she admitted that of which she was accused, she said, 'I admit, my dear lords', and she added, 'Here I stand, I cannot speak differently. May God help me.' The judges crowded together to collect the votes. Nogod said, 'It is, indeed, true what this wench sayeth, but what business had she to gossip about it thus? If we let it pass, she will use her jaw against us also. I speak in favour of her being punished.' Lovestrife said, 'Certainly, if one was let off such a thing, others would also ask for forbearance.' Hearsay said, 'I do not truly know what has happened; but as Spiteful lays so much importance on this matter, I conclude that it really gives him pain; let her then be punished.' Partial said, 'I had known before this that this gossip blurts out all she knows; it is necessary to stop her jaws.' Loveself said, 'The injured man is my good friend. She should at least have spared him, for my sake, instead of gibing at him in this fashion; she deserves punishment.' Lovegold said, 'You all know how generous Spiteful has proved himself; he de-serves our protection.' Takegift said, 'It is so; we would be ungrateful if his suit were lost.' Ignorant said, 'I know no precedent in this case. Let her suffer as she has deserved.' Then Knowlittle, 'I do not understand the case. I agree to whatever sentence you may pass.' Dontcare said, 'Be it is as it may. I accede to everything.' Dilatory said, 'Can we not defer the law suit? Perhaps the matter will clear itself up later.' Hasty said, 'Not so; let us pass judgement while we are so minded.' The Chief Justice said, 'Certainly; whom have we to consider? As the law wills it, so it must be done.' And rising he delivered his sentence, 'As this pratt-ling woman has given herself up to such unbecoming conduct as to pester good men, she shall receive forty slaps in the face save one for the taming of her unbridled tongue and as a warning unto others. This is our pronouncement against her.' Thereupon Spiteful with his counsel and witnesses bowed and gave thanks for this just finding. Simplicity was also urged to do so, but she gave herself up to crying and wringing of hands. Thereupon because she did not respect the court the punishment was increased and they led her away to punishment. Seeing the injustice that had been done to her I could not restrain myself and exclaimed aloud, 'Oh, if all tribunals in the world are as this one, may God the Almighty so help me that I may never become a judge or go to law with anyone !' 'Be silent, madman', said the interpreter and he placed his fist before my mouth, 'On my oath I say that thou shalt talk thyself into the same as or even worse punishment than this woman.' And, indeed, Spiteful and Flattery began to bring forward witnesses against me ; perceiving this and becoming alarmed I flew out of the place all out of breath scarcely knowing how.

6. While I took breath outside the court-house and wiped my eyes, I saw many coming to the courts bringing plaints and the advocates Babbler, Flatterer, Mislead, Procrastination and others running to meet them, offering their services, but considering not so much what plaint but what purse each man had. Each man carried with him his own law book busily (the which I had not noticed among the theologians) and sometimes searched in it. Now, on some of these books I saw inscriptions such as 'The Devouring Torment of the Land', or 'The Rapacious Defraudment of the Land'. Unable to look at this any longer, I went away sighing.

7. Searchall said to me, 'The best yet remains. Come and behold the rule of kings, princes and others who reign over their subjects by hereditary right; perhaps this will please thee.' And we went into another place, and behold, men sat there on chairs that were so high and broad that but few could approach or reach them save by means of contrivances. Each one instead of ears had long tubes on both sides, and those who wished to say something had to whisper into them. But they were crooked and full of holes, and many words were lost before they reached the head, and those that reached it were mostly altered. For that reason, as I noticed, not all that spoke received an answer; at times even when one clamoured very loudly the sound did not penetrate to the brain of the ruler; sometimes, again, an answer was given, but it was not to the point. Similarly instead of the eyes and the tongue there were tubes, and seen through them, things often appeared different from what they really were, and answers were given that differed from the intentions of the ruler himself. Understanding this, I said, 'Why, then, do they not put away these tubes and see, hear, answer with their own eyes, ears, tongue

as plain people do ?' 'Because of the preciousness of their person and the dignity of their rank', said the interpreter, 'there must be such circumlocutions; or dost thou think they are peasants whose eyes, ears, and mouth everyone may pester ?'

8. Just then I perceived some who walked round the thrones; of these some by means of these tubes were breathing into the ears of their master; others placed spectacles of one or another colour before his eyes; others burnt incense before his nose; others guided his hands in folding and unfolding, others directed his feet binding and loosening them; others adjusted and strengthened the throne under him, and so forth. Seeing this, I asked, 'Who are these ? And what do they ?' The interpreter answered, 'They are the privy councillors who instruct the king and great lords.' 'I should not', quoth I, 'allow this if I were in their position; rather should I wish to have freedom of my own limbs and actions.' He answered, 'A single man must not take everything on himself nor should he be allowed to do so.' Then said I, 'These great lords are more wretched than peasants being so bound that they cannot even move except in accordance with the will of others.' 'Yet are they more certain of themselves', said he; 'Look at these !'

9. And I looked round, and behold some of those who sat on these chairs did not allow themselves to be ordered about, and drove these advisers from them, and this was according to my liking. But here I immediately found other evils. In the place of the few that had been driven away there came many others and they tried to breathe into the ears, nose, and mouth of the ruler, to cover and uncover his eyes in divers fashions; to stretch out his hands and feet now in this, now in that direction; every newcomer tried to push and pull him to the side on which he himself happened to be standing until the unhappy lord knew not what to do; to whom he should give way, who he should resist, nor how he could be a match for them all. And I said, 'I see already that it is better to trust to a few chosen ones than to be the prey of them all; but could not all this be contrived somewhat differently ?' 'And how could it be contrived ?' quoth he; 'The estate of the ruler compels him to receive complaints, accusations, petitions, appeals, arguments and counter-arguments from all, and to render everyone his just due unless they are like these other princes.'

10. Then he pointed to some lords who allowed nobody near them except such as ministered to and worked for their comfort. And I saw that they had around them men who were skipping about like servants,

stroking them, propping them up with pillows, placing mirrors before their eyes, cooling them with fans, picking up the feathers and sweeping, kissing their garments and shoes, all this in front of their faces; some even licked the spittle and snivel that came forth from their masters, praising it as being sweet. But all this, again, pleased me not; in particular when I saw that the throne of almost every one of these rulers tottered, and, before he knew it, overturned, when he lacked the more trusty supporters.

11. Now it befell in my presence that a royal throne began to totter and broke into bits, and the ruler fell to the ground. Immediately a crowd of people gathered, and as I watched them, I saw that they were leading another prince and seating him on the throne, while they joyously declared that things would now be different from what they had been before; thereupon everyone pranced about him, supported and strengthened the new throne as much as they could. Now I, thinking it well to act for the common welfare (for thus they called it), came nearer and contributed a nail or two to strengthen the new throne; for this some praised me, while others looked askance at me. But meanwhile the other prince, having gathered his men, fell upon us with cudgels, thrashing the whole crowd, till they all fled and many even lost their necks. I was so panic-stricken that I hardly knew what to do till my companion Searchall, hearing them inquire as to 'Who had aided and abetted the other prince', nudged me that I also might flee. Delusion said that it was not necessary; whereupon I, while reflecting which of them to obey, was grazed by a cudgel which was brandished near, and gathering myself together ran into a corner to hide. Thus I came to understand that to sit on these chairs or to be near them, or indeed to touch them in any way, was dangerous. Therefore I preferred to go away from here, and resolved never again to return. And accordingly I spoke to my guides, 'Let him who will approach these heights, but not I.'

12. And I was yet more certain because I discovered that though all those people wished to be called rulers of the world, misrule was rampant everywhere. For whether the prince dealt with his subjects through tubes, or whether he delivered his decrees by means of the whispers of others, I saw as much evil as justice, I heard as much groaning and lamentation as merriment, and that justice with injustice and violence with legality were intermingled; that the town halls, the law courts, the chanceries were as much the workshops of injustice as justice, and that those who call themselves defenders of order in the world are as much

(and often more) the defenders of disorder than order. And wondering how much vanity and glittering misery is concealed within this estate, I took leave of these men and went away.

Chapter XX

Soldiery

We then entered the last street, and in the first market-place a crowd of men clothed in red were standing about; approaching them I heard that they were deliberating among themselves as to how they could give wings to Death so that she could in a moment penetrate everywhere both near and far; item, how that which had been built during many years could be destroyed in an hour. And I became afeared on hearing such speech; for hitherto what I had learned of human labour, concerned the education and the increase of mankind, only strove for furthering human comfort, but these deliberated on the destruction of the lives and of the comforts of men. The interpreter answered, 'The endeavours of these men also tend to that purpose but by a somewhat different path— to wit, they remove that which is harmful. Later thou wilt understand.'

2. Meanwhile we came to a gate where instead of gate-keepers there stood a number of drummers who asked each one who wished to enter whether he had a purse. When he showed and opened it, they poured silver into it and said, 'Your skin is paid for', and then they took him to a cellar, and afterwards conducted him out, equipped with iron and fire, and ordered him to proceed farther into the market-place.

3. And I desired to see what was in this vault, so I immediately entered. And behold there lay there on the ground on all sides without end

IOHAN·AMOS COMENIVS·MORAVVS·A° ÆTAT 50. 164

Ex sump: M: S: G. Glouer: fe:

Loe, here an Exile! who to serue his God,
Hath sharply tasted of proud Pashurs Rod;
Whose learning, Piety, & true worth, being knowne
To all the world, makes all the world his owne.
                                                    F.Q.

Portrait of J. A. Comenius, by J. Glouer.

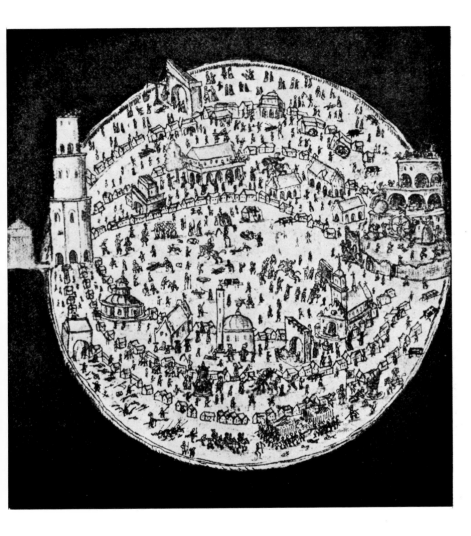

Sketch of a town by J. A. Comenius which appeared in the original manuscript of *The Labyrinth of the World and the Paradise of the Heart*; the original of this sketch is in the Library of the National Museum in Prague.

piled to enormous heights that thousands of carts could not have trans-
ported, heaps of all kinds of cruel weapons for stabbing, chopping, cut-
ting, piercing, pricking, hacking, stinging, severing, tearing, burning, in
a word instruments for destroying life made of iron, lead, wood, and
stone, that terror befell me, and I said, 'Against what wild beasts are
they preparing these things?' 'Against men', the interpreter answered.
'Against men!' quoth I, 'Alas! I had thought against some mad animal
or wild, furious beasts. But, in the name of God, what cruelty this is,
if men devise such terrible things against men!' 'Art thou so fastidious?'
he said, laughing.

4. And going onward, we proceeded to a market-place where I saw
these men who were clothed in iron, and had horns and claws, and were
fettered together in herds; they were crouching before what seemed
troughs and jugs into which their food and drink had been thrown down
and poured, and out of which they vied with each other to gobble and
lap it up. And I said, 'Are hogs being here fattened for butchery? I see
indeed the likenesses of men but swinish deeds.' 'That is the advantage
of this estate', said the interpreter. Meanwhile they rose from these
troughs and gave themselves to frolics and dancing, skipping and shouting. Whereupon the interpreter said, 'Well, dost thou see the delights of
this life? What do they have to worry about? Is it not merry to be here?'
'I shall wait for what will befall later', said I. But they now began to
pursue and harry every man whom they met who was not of their own
estate. Then wallowing on the earth, they committed sodomy and every
infamy without any shame or fear of God, till I blushed and said,
'Surely this they should not be allowed to do.' 'They must be allowed',
said the interpreter, 'for this estate claims every kind of liberty.' They
then sat down and began to gobble again and after they had crammed
themselves with food and drink until they were speechless, they fell to
the ground and began to snore. Then they were led into the market-
place where rain, snow, hail, frost, sleet, thirst, hunger, and every sort
of evil rained on them, then no few trembled, shook, pined away,
perished—the food of all dogs and crows. Yet others heeded not and
continued to revel.

5. Suddenly the drums beat and the trumpets resounded, and tumult
and shouting broke out; then behold all rose up, seized dirks, cutlasses,
daggers, or whatever they had, and began to plunge them into each other
till the blood spurted, for they cut and hacked at one another worse than
the most savage animals. Then a deafening din spread in all directions;

one could hear the trampling of horses, the clashing of armour, the clattering of swords, the growl of the artillery, the whistle of shots and bullets round our ears, the sound of trumpets, the crash of drums, the cries of these who urged on the battle, the shouting of the victors, the shrieking of the wounded and dying. An awful leaden hailstorm could be seen; dreadful fiery thunder and lightning could be heard; now this, now that man's arm, head, leg flew away; here one fell over the other all writhing in blood. 'Almighty God', quoth I, 'What is happening, must the whole world perish?'

Hardly had my spirits somewhat recovered, but scarcely knowing how and where I was, I fled this spot; then after somewhat regaining my breath, I said though still trembling to my guides, 'Whither have you led me?' The interpreter answered, 'Out upon thee, you milksop! To be able to fight others that is what makes a man of you.' 'What have they done to each other?' I said. He answered, 'The lords fell out and then the matter had to be settled.' 'What! Do these men settle it?' quoth I. He answered, 'Certainly, for who could make great lords, kings and king-doms that have no judge above them agree? They must decide the differ-ences between them by means of the sword. He who surpasses the other in the use of sword and fire prevails.' 'Oh, barbarity, oh, beastliness!' quoth I. 'Was there no other way to reconcile them? Wild beasts should thus settle their differences, not men.'

6. Just then I saw that they led and carried from the battlefield many with severed hands, arms, head, nose, with riddled bodies, tattered skins, and all bespattered with blood. While I could from pity scarcely look at them, the interpreter said, 'All this will heal; a soldier must be hardy.' 'What of those', I said, 'who lost their lives?' He answered, 'Their hides had already been paid for.' 'How this?' said I. 'Hast thou not seen how many pleasant things were previously granted them?' 'And what un-pleasant things had they also to endure?' quoth I; 'And even if only delights had previously been their lot, it is a wretched thing to give food to a man only that he may be forced to go to the shambles directly after-wards. It is an ugly estate in any case. I like it not! I like it not! Let us go hence.'

[Translated from the Czech by Mrs. Iris Urwin.]

The Great Didactic

The *Great Didactic* was first written by Comenius in Czech. Then when all hope of educational reform in Bohemia had vanished, he translated the work into Latin and added Chapters XXVIII to XXXIII. He was still living in his own country when *The Great Didactic* was begun in 1627; the Latin version was completed in 1638, but was published for the first time in Amsterdam in 1657, at the head of the great collection of didactic works entitled *Opera Didactica Omnia*.

In Comenius' day, schools were the subject of general dissatisfaction. Education was considered to give only bookish, verbal knowledge; it was unsystematic, owing to the chaotic state of school organization, and unmethodical, because teachers were insufficiently trained and adopted out-of-date practices. Comenius realized that the situation could not be permanently remedied by changes of detail. The root of the evil lay in the fact that instruction was not in harmony with human nature or with man's role in the universe. His book was therefore conceived as a philosophy of education; although he entered fully into practical details, he handled his subject systematically. It was a first step in the preparation of 'pansophic' schemes which were intended to reform all human affairs by means of education.

The Great Didactic opens with an analysis of man's place in the world of which he is the summit. Everything grows in nature; man likewise must grow and improve through education, the laws of which may be determined, thanks to the universal harmony governing the relationship between nature and art. Education must begin very early; it must be continuous and not coercive, after the example of natural development. All children, irrespective of sex or economic and social position, must receive it. Comenius criticizes the faults of the schools of his day, and gives advice on how to avoid them. He discusses, not merely language teaching itself, but also the various basic disciplines necessarily underlying it. A curriculum is offered for education in the home, in primary school, in Latin school and, lastly, at the academy, after which time young people are to complete their training by travel.

The Great Didactic is regarded as the classic work upon which every type of systematic teaching is based. It has been translated into almost all the main languages, and often more than once (see the bibliography at the end of this volume).

The passages here quoted concern methods for the rapid, rational teaching of sciences and languages alike. They are taken from the central section of the book, which describes the 'natural' methods of instruction, based on the idea of a parallel between nature and art.

Chapter XIX

The Principles of Conciseness and Rapidity in Teaching

'But these projects are too wearisome and too comprehensive', many readers will here remark. 'What a number of teachers and of libraries, and how much labour will be necessary in order for such universal education to be given!' I answer: This is undoubtedly so, and unless our labours are shortened the task will be no easy one; for this art of ours is as long, as wide, and as deep as the universe that has to be subdued by our minds. But who does not know that diffuse and difficult things can be brought into a small compass? Who is ignorant that weavers can weave together a hundred thousand threads with the greatest rapidity, and can produce from these a great variety of stuffs? Or that millers can grind thousands of grains with the greatest ease, and can separate the bran from the flour with great exactness and without any difficulty? Everyone knows that handicraftsmen, without the slightest trouble and with comparatively small machines, can raise enormous weights, and that a weight of one ounce, if at a sufficient distance from the fulcrum of a lever, can counterbalance many pounds.

We see, therefore, that great achievements are more often a question of skill than of strength. Are learned men then to be the only people who do not know how to conduct their affairs with skill? Surely shame should compel us to emulate the inventive spirit of other professions and find a remedy for the difficulties with which schools have hitherto struggled.

2. It is impossible to find a remedy until we have discovered the diseases and their causes. What can it be that has impeded the efforts of the schools and hindered their success to such an extent that many, although they have spent a whole life in school, do not traverse the whole range of the sciences and arts, while some of them scarely even cross the threshold?

3. The causes of this are undoubtedly the following: firstly, no fixed landmarks were set up, which might serve as goals to be reached by the

scholars at the end of each year, month, or day, therefore, there was no system in anything.

4. Secondly, the roads that would infallibly lead to these goals were not pointed out.

5. Thirdly, things that should naturally be associated were not joined together, but were kept apart. For instance, the scholars in elementary schools were taught to read, but were not given lessons in writing till some months afterwards. In the Latin School boys were allowed to spend some years in learning words without any reference to objects, so that their boyhood was wholly occupied by grammatical studies, and all philosophic interest was reserved for a later period. In the same way the scholars were only allowed to learn, never to teach, though all these things (reading and writing, words and things, learning and teaching) should be associated, just as, in running, the raising of the feet is combined with the setting of them on the ground again, or, in conversation, listening is combined with answering, or, in playing ball, throwing is combined with catching as we have seen above in the relevant passage.

6. Fourthly, the arts and the sciences were scarcely ever taught as part of an encyclopaedic whole, but were dealt out piecemeal. This has been the reason why, in the eyes of the scholars, they seemed like a heap of wood or of faggots, in which the exact connexion and combining links can scarcely be discerned. Thus it came to pass that some grasped one fact, others another, and that none received a really thorough and universal education.

7. Fifthly, many different methods were employed. Each school and even each teacher used a different one. What was worse, teachers would use one method in one subject or language, and another in another, and, worst of all, even in one individual subject they varied their method, so that the scholar scarcely understood in what way he was expected to learn. Hence arose the hesitation and delay, the distaste for and lack of confidence in new subjects even before they had been begun, so that many even had no interest in attempting them.

8. Sixthly, no method was known by which instruction could be given to all the pupils in a class at the same time; the teacher worked to teach only the individual scholar. With a large number of pupils this must have been an impossible task for the teacher. For the scholars it was the occasion for useless idleness or burdensome work if each was given some exercise until his turn came.

9. Seventhly, if there were several teachers, this was a fresh source of

confusion; since each hour some new subject was introduced. Not to mention the fact that a diversity of teachers tends to distract the mind quite as much as a diversity of books.

10. Finally, both in school and out of it, the scholars had perfect freedom as regards the books they read, and the teachers gave them no assistance in their choice. For all were imbued with the idea that to read many authors afforded many opportunities of making progress, whereas such diversity produced nothing but distraction. It was not surprising, therefore, that very few mastered all the branches of study. The wonder was that any one was able to find his way out of such a labyrinth—and indeed only the most gifted succeeded in doing so.

11. For the future, therefore, hindrances and delays of this sort must be set aside, and we must make straight for our goal, neglecting everything that is not of immediate service. As the saying goes: 'Where small means suffice, great should not be used.'

12. Let us choose the sun for imitation, since it affords a striking example of the operations of nature. Its functions are laborious and almost unlimited (namely, to send forth its rays over the whole world and to supply all the elements, minerals, plants, and animals, of which countless species exist, with light, warmth, life, and strength), but it proves equal to them all, and every year fulfils the circle of its duties in the most admirable manner.

13. We will therefore examine its various principles of action, with reference to the above-mentioned desiderata of school management.

(i) The sun does not occupy itself with any single object, animal, or tree; but lights and warms the whole earth at once.

(ii) It gives light to all things with the same rays; covers all things with moisture by the same processes of evaporation and condensation; it causes the same wind to blow on all things; it puts all things in motion by the same warmth and cold.

(iii) It causes spring, summer, autumn, and winter to make their appearance in all lands at the same time. Through its agency, the trees grow green, blossom, and bear fruit (though some do so earlier than others, each according to its nature).

(iv) It always preserves the same order; one day resembles another, one year resembles the next. It always operates on one object by the same method.

(v) It produces everything from its elementary form, and from no other source.

(vi) It produces in combination everything that ought to be combined; wood with its bark and its core, a flower with its leaves, a fruit with its skin and its stalk.

(vii) It causes everything to develop through definite stages, so that one stage prepares the way for the next, and each stage follows naturally from the previous one.

(viii) Finally, it brings into existence nothing that is useless, or destroys such an object if it be accidentally produced.

14. In imitation of this:

(i) There should only be one teacher in each school, or at any rate in each class.

(ii) Only one author should be used for each subject studied.

(iii) The same exercise should be given to the whole class.

(iv) All subjects and languages should be taught by the same method.

(v) Everything should be taught thoroughly, briefly, and pithily, that the understanding may be, as it were, unlocked by one key, and may then unravel fresh difficulties of its own accord.

(vi) All things that are naturally connected ought to be taught in combination.

(vii) Every subject shoud be taught in definitely graded steps, that the work of one day may thus expand that of the previous day, and lead up to that of the morrow.

(viii) And finally, everything that is useless should be invariably discarded.

15. If these reforms could be introduced into schools, there is no doubt that the whole circle of the sciences might be completed with an ease that surpasses our expectation, just as the sun completes its circling course through the heavens every year. Let us therefore get to work and see if these counsels can be carried into effect, and how the difficulties that hinder their realisation can be overcome.

First Problem

How can a single teacher teach a number of boys, no matter how great, at one time ?

16. I maintain that it is not only possible for one teacher to teach several hundred scholars at once, but that it is also essential; since for both the teachers and their pupils it is by far the most advantageous

system. The larger the number of pupils that he sees before him the greater the interest the teacher will take in his work (just as the hands of a miner tremble with excitement when he discovers a rich vein of ore); and the keener the teacher himself, the greater the enthusiasm that his pupils will display. To the scholars, in the same way, the presence of a number of companions will be productive not only of utility but also of enjoyment (for it gives pleasure to all to have companions in their labour); since they will mutually stimulate and assist one another. Indeed for boys of this age emulation is by far the best stimulus. Again, if a teacher's class be small, this point or that may escape the ears of all his pupils. But if many hear him at once, each one grasps as much as he can, and then, when the lesson is repeated, all comes back into their minds again, since one mind has an invigorating effect on another and one memory on another. In short, as a baker makes a large quantity of bread by a single kneading of the dough and a single heating of the oven, as a brick-maker burns many bricks at one time, as a printer prints hundreds of thousands of books from the same set of type, so should a teacher be able to teach a very large number of pupils at once and without the slightest inconvenience. Do we not see that one trunk can support innumerable branches and supply them with sap, and that the sun is able to vivify the whole earth?

17. How is this to be done? Let us take our former examples, and watch the processes of nature. The trunk does not extend to the outermost branches, but remaining in its place supplies sap to the large ones that are in immediate connexion with it, these pass it on to others, and these again in their turn to others, and so on until the smallest twigs have been reached. In the same way the sun does not illumine each individual tree, plant, or animal, but, sending forth its rays from on high, lights up half the world at once, and thus supplies each creature with light and warmth for its own use. We should here notice that the sun's action may be assisted by the lie of the ground, because the rays that collect in the valleys give a higher degree of warmth to this region.

18. If matters be arranged in the following manner, one teacher will easily be able to cope with a very large number of scholars. That is to say:

(i) If he divide the whole body into classes, groups of ten, for example, each of which should be controlled by a scholar who is, in his turn, controlled by one of higher rank, and so on.

(ii) If he never give individual instruction, either privately out of school or publicly in school, but teach all the pupils at one and the same

5

time. He should, therefore, never step up to any one scholar or allow any one of them to come to him separately, but should remain in his seat, where he can be seen and heard by all, just as the sun sends forth its rays over all things. The scholars, on the other hand, must direct their ears, eyes, and thoughts towards him and attend to everything that he tells them by word of mouth or explains by means of his hand or of diagrams. Thus, with a single blow, not one but many flies are killed.

19. With a little skill it will be possible to arrest the attention of the pupils, collectively and individually, and to imbue them with the notion that (as really is the case) the mouth of the teacher is a spring from which streams of knowledge issue and flow over them, and that, whenever they see this spring open, they should place their attention, like a cistern, beneath it, and thus allow nothing that flows forth to escape. The teacher also should take the greatest care never to speak unless all his pupils are listening, nor to teach unless they are all attending. In this connexion that remark of Seneca's is very apposite: 'We should speak to none who is unwilling to listen.' Solomon also says: 'Wisdom is before him that hath understanding' (Prov. XVII. 24). That is to say, we should talk not to the winds but to the ears of men.

20. It is not solely by means of the leaders, or of the other boys in charge, that attention can be awakened and retained. The teacher is himself the most important factor, and will succeed in his efforts if he observe eight rules.

(i) If, when he teaches, he take the trouble continually to introduce something that is entertaining as well as of practical use; for in this way the interest of the scholars will be excited and their attention will be arrested.

(ii) If, at the commencement of any new subject, he excite the interest of his pupils, either by placing it before them in an attractive manner or by asking them questions. These latter may either refer to what has preceded, and thus illustrate the connexion between it and the subject in question, or to the new branch of study. For, if the scholar's ignorance of the subject be mercilessly exposed, he may be fired with a desire to master it and understand it thoroughly.

(iii) If he stand on an elevated platform, and, keeping all the scholars in his sight at once, allow none of them to do anything but attend and look at him.

(iv) If he aid their attention by appealing to the senses, especially to that of sight, whenever it is possible (as we have shown above,

Chap. XVII, in the third rule of the eighth Principle). For this not only assists in simplifying things but also in holding the attention.

(v) If he occasionally interrupt this explanation with the words: Tell me (mentioning some boy), what have I just said? Repeat that sentence! Tell me; how have I reached this point? and remarks of a similar kind, the exact nature of which must depend on the class that he is teaching. If any pupil be found who is not paying attention, he should be reprimanded or punished on the spot. In this way the scholars will be made keen and attentive.

(vi) Similarly, if he ask one boy, and he hesitate, he should pass on to a second, a third, a tenth, or a thirtieth, and ask for the answer without repeating the question. The result of this will be that all listen carefully to what is said to one of their number, and apply it to their own use.

(vii) If some of the boys cannot answer a question he should ask the whole class, and then, in the presence of the rest, praise those who answer first or best, that their example may serve to stimulate the others. If any pupil make a mistake he should be corrected, but at the same time the cause of the error (which a clever teacher will have no difficulty in discovering) should be made clear and the necessity for its recurrence obviated. It can scarcely be realized what an assistance to rapid progress this will be.

(viii) Finally, when the lesson is over, the scholars should be given leave to ask questions on any point that they wish explained, because they query something either in the present lesson or in a previous one. Private questioning should not be permitted. Each scholar who wishes to ask a question should either ask the teacher openly or get the leader of his division to do so (if this latter is unable to solve the difficulty himself). In this way the whole class will benefit, and as much by the question as by the answer. If any scholar help several times to illustrate an important point by the intelligence of his questions, he should be commended, in order that the rest may thereby be incited to industry and keenness.

21. Such a daily training of the attention will not only be of momentary use to the young, but will stand them in good stead throughout their whole lives. For if this training last for some years, and they get into the habit of concentrating their minds on whatever is being done at the time, they will continue to do so of their own accord without any external pressure. If schools are organized on this principle, surely we may look forward to a considerable increase in the number of clever and intelligent men.

22. To this it may be objected that individual attention is necessary to see that each scholar keeps his books tidy, writes his exercises carefully, and learns his lessons accurately, and that, if the class be large, this will take a great deal of time. I answer: It is not necessary for the teacher always to hear the lessons or inspect the books of each individual scholar; since he has the leaders of divisions to assist him, and each of these can see that the scholars in his own division do everything properly.

23. The teacher, as chief inspector, should give his attention first to one scholar, then to another, more particularly with the view of testing the honesty of those whom he distrusts. For example, if the scholars have to say a repetition lesson, he should call first on one pupil, then on another, first one at the top of the class and then one at the bottom, while all the rest attend. He may thus ensure that each one be in readiness, since none can be certain that he will not be examined. If the teacher observe that a scholar begins his lessons without hesitation, and feel convinced that he knows the rest equally well, he may let another one go on, and if this one in turn seem well prepared, may pass on to a third. In this way, by hearing a few, he can rest assured that he has the whole class under his control.

24. The same method should be pursued with dictations if there are any. One or more scholars should read out what has been written, with the right punctuation and in a clear voice, while the rest correct what they have written in their books. The teacher should also himself examine the books sometimes at random and should punish any scholar who has been doing his work carelessly.

25. The correction of written exercise seems to demand more time; but here also the same method may be adopted with advantage. For example in translation exercises from one language into another the following method should be used: as soon as the leaders of divisions have secured attention, one scholar should be called upon to stand up and choose as his adversary any other scholar that he pleases. As soon as this latter stands up, the first scholar reads out his translation sentence by sentence, while all the rest listen attentively, the teacher (or at any rate the leader) in the meantime looking at the exercise to see that it is properly written. At the end of each sentence the scholar stops, and his adversary has the opportunity of pointing out any mistake that he may have perceived. Then other scholars in the division, and after them the whole class, may make criticisms on the rendering, and finally the teacher supplies any point that has been omitted. Meanwhile all the scholars

look into their own exercise books and, if they have made a similar mistake, they correct it. The adversary, however, should not do so, but should keep his own unaltered that he may submit it to the criticism of his companions. As soon as the first sentence has been properly corrected, the next is taken, and so on until the exercise is finished. Then the adversary should read out his in the same way, while the original challenger takes care that he really reads his original translation and does not insert the corrections that have been made. The individual words and phrases are then criticised as before. After this, a second pair of adversaries is chosen, and the same procedure is repeated for as long as the time permits.

26. In this connexion the leaders have two duties to perform. Before the corrections begin they should see that all the scholars have their exercises ready, and while it is going on they should take care that each of them corrects his exercise when it contains the mistake that is under consideration.

27. The result of this will be:

(i)   That the work of the teacher will be lightened.

(ii) That all scholars will be taught, and none neglected.

(iii) That the scholars will attend better than formerly.

(iv) That what is said to one will be of equal advantage to all.

(v)   The differences in the mode of expression, that are certain to be used by different scholars, will not only improve and strengthen the scholar's acquaintance with the subject-matter, but will also give him facility in using the language.

(vi) Finally, as soon as the first, second, and third pair have finished, it will frequently happen that the others have few or no mistakes left to correct. When this is the case, the remainder of the time may be devoted to the class in general; those who are still uncertain about a passage may bring forward their difficulties, or those who think that their rendering is better than that which has been given may read it and receive criticism on it.

28. The method here suggested has been illustrated by an exercise in translation. Its application, however, is just as easy, if the exercise be one in style, rhetoric, logic, theology, or philosophy.

29. We have thus seen that one teacher can instruct a hundred scholars with as little labour as he would expend in teaching a few.

Second Problem

How is it possible for all the scholars to be taught from the same books ?

30. It is an undisputed fact that too many objects at once distract the attention. It will therefore be of immense advantage if the scholars be allowed to use no books but those that have been expressly composed for the class in which they are; and in this way it will always be possible to use with effect the order that was given to the worshippers in the temples of old, namely, 'This shalt thou do.' Since the less the eyes are distracted, the easier it is to concentrate the mind.

31. Secondly, if all the materials that are required for instruction, blackboards, inscriptions, first reading books, dictionaries, schematic diagrams of the arts, etc., be kept in constant readiness. For if (as is often the case) the teacher must prepare the list of the alphabet for the scholars, and write a model for them to copy, or if he have to dictate grammatical rules, the text of an author, or its translation, how much time is thereby lost! It is therefore necessary that sufficient quantities of all the books which are used in each class be kept in readiness, and that translations be supplied with those texts that are to be translated into the mother-tongue. In this way the time that would otherwise have been employed in dictation, copying, and translating, can be used, and with far greater advantage, for explanation, repetition, and imitation.

32. There need be no fear that any concession is here being made to the teacher's idleness. For a preacher is considered to have done his duty if he read a text from the Bible, explain it, and point out its application (for instruction, admonition, pleasure, etc.) and it is a matter of indifference to his hearers whether he has himself translated the text from the original, or has used some standard translation; and in the same way it makes no difference to the scholars whether the teacher has arranged his own materials or whether some one else has done so for him. The important thing is that everything necessary be ready to hand, and that, under the teacher's direction, it be properly employed. It is indeed much better that everything of this nature be prepared beforehand, since, on the one hand, it will be freer from errors, and, on the other, more time will be left for the actual process of practical exercises.

33. For every school, therefore, books of this kind should be written—in accordance with the rules already laid down for the attainment of ease, thoroughness, and economy of time—and should constitute a

complete, thorough, and accurate epitome of all the subjects of instruction. In short, they should give a true representation of the entire universe, which can thus be impressed upon the minds of the scholars. They should also, and this is a most important point, be written simply and clearly, and should give the scholars sufficient assistance to enable them, if necessary, to understand everything without the help of a teacher.

34. With this end in view it is desirable that they be written in the form of a dialogue. In this way (1) it is possible to suit the subject-matter and its exposition to the minds of the young, that they should not imagine things as impossible, incomprehensible, or too difficult. Nothing is more suited to inspire confidence than dialogue-form, and by means of it the mind can be gradually led on unawares to the desired goal. It is in this form that playwrights have expressed their views on the deterioration of morals, and have thereby admonished the people; in this form Plato wrote all his philosophical, and St. Augustine all his theological works, and Cicero also has employed it largely, thus coming down to the level of his readers. (2) Conversational form excites and retains the attention, while the alternation between question and answer, the various forms of expression and the amusing remarks that may be introduced, and even the changes that may be rung upon the dramatis personae, all tend, not merely to counteract any antipathy to the subject, but even to create a keen desire to know more about it. (3) Instruction makes a far greater impression when given in this way. We remember an event better when we have seen it ourselves than when we have simply heard it narrated, and, in the same way, instruction that is given through the medium of a drama or of a dialogue stays in the heads of the scholars far better than if it be merely set forth by a teacher in the ordinary way, as may be proved by experience (for it seems to us that in this case we see more readily than we hear). (4) The greater part of our lives consists of friendly conversation, and it should therefore be easy to induce the young to acquire useful information, when they are at the same time learning to express themselves fluently, readily and seriously. (5) Finally, dialogues of this kind make repetition easier, and may enliven the private gatherings of the students.

35. It is also desirable that the books used be of the same edition, so that they may be similar page for page and line for line. This is important both for the sake of reference and that the localization of passages on certain pages may assist the memory.

36. It will also be of great use if an abstract of the contents of all the books used in the class be placed on the walls of the room. This should consist of the text, greatly abbreviated and condensed, or of illustrative pictures and reliefs, by means of which the senses, the memory, and the understanding may be daily exercised in conjunction. Not without purpose was it that, as the ancients relate, the walls of the temple of Aesculapius were covered with the precepts of the art of medicine, and that Hippocrates entered in secret and copied them down. This great theatre of the world, also, God has filled with pictures, statues, and living emblems of His wisdom, that He may instruct us by their means. (Of these pictorial aids we will say more when we treat of the individual classes.)

Third Problem

How is it possible for all the scholars in a school to do the same thing at one time?

37. It is evident that it would be a useful arrangement if all the pupils in a class did the same lesson at one time, for in this way the teacher would have less trouble and the scholars greater advantage. It is only when the attention of all is fixed on the same object, and when each tries in turn to correct the other, that keen rivalry can arise. In every way the teacher must imitate a captain of recruits. This latter does not exercise each of his men separately, but leads out a whole company at once and shows them how to use their arms; and even if he explain anything to one man apart, the remainder have to go through the same exercise in order that their attention may be retained. The teacher should proceed on precisely similar lines.

38. Before he can do this it is necessary:

(i) That the course of instruction commence at one definite time in each year, just as the influence of the sun on the vegetable world commences at one definite time, namely, in spring.

(ii) That the subject of instruction be so divided that each year, each month, each week, each day, and even each hour may have a definite task appointed for it, since, if this be done, everything that is proposed will be completed with ease. But of this we will say more in the proper place.

Fourth Problem

How is it possible to teach everything according to one and the same method?

39. That there is only one natural method for all the sciences, and only one for all the arts and languages, will be shown in Chapters XX, XXI, and XXII. Any deviations that may be necessary are not important enough to constitute a fresh class, and are due less to peculiarities in the subject-matter than to the teacher himself, who must be guided by the ability, or the reverse, of his pupils and by the progress that they make in the actual languages or arts that he is teaching. The universal adoption of the natural method, therefore, will be as great a boon to scholars as a plain and undeviating road is to travellers. It will be easier to remember special aberrations if they are pointed out separately, provided that what is general and universal remains intact.

Fifth Problem

How can many things be explained in a few words?

40. To fill the minds of scholars with a dreary waste of books and of words is lost labour. For it is certain that a crust of bread and a mouthful of wine are more nutritious than a paunchful of trifle and of ragout, and that it is better to have a few gold pieces in one's purse than a hundredweight of lead. Rightly does Seneca say of instruction: 'Its administration should resemble the sowing of seed, in which stress is laid, not on quantity, but on quality.' The conclusion, therefore, that we reached in Chapter V holds good: In man, the microcosm, everything is contained potentially. Bring light and he will straightway see. And indeed for men who are working in the dark the faintest glimmer of light is sufficient. It is therefore necessary to select or to write handbooks of the sciences and languages which are small in compass and practically arranged—cover the whole subject and contain a great deal of matter in a short space (Ecclesiasticus, XXXII. 8)—that is to say, which place before the scholar the whole of the subject-matter by means of a small number of rules and definitions expressed in the simplest and clearest language, and sufficient in themselves to make all other things easily comprehensible.

Sixth Problem

How is it possible to do two or three things by a single operation?

41. The examples in nature show that several things can be done at one time and by means of the same operation. It is an undoubted fact that a tree grows above the ground and beneath it at the same time, and that its wood, its bark, its leaves, and its fruits, all develop simultaneously. The same observation applies to animals, whose limbs all develop and grow stronger at the same time. Further, each limb performs several operations. The feet, for instance, not only support a man but also move him forwards and backwards in various ways. The mouth is not only the entrance to the body, but also serves as a masticator and as a trumpet that sounds whenever called upon to do so. With a single inspiration the lungs cool the heart, purify the brain, and assist in voice production.

42. We find the same thing in the arts: (1) In the sun-dial, the single shadow cast by the gnomon points out the hour of the day, the sign of the zodiac in which the sun is moving, the length of the day and of the night, the day of the month, and several other things (even according to various ways of reckoning time). (2) One pole serves to direct, to turn, and to hold back a carriage. (3) A good orator or writer instructs, excites and pleases at the same time, although these three elements differ from each other so much.

43. The instruction of the young should be similarly organized, so that every activity may produce several results. It may be laid down as a general rule that each subject should be taught in combination with those which are correlative to it; that is to say, words should be studied in combination with the things to which they refer; while reading and writing, exercises in style and in logical thought, teaching and learning, amusement and serious study and whatever else it may be possible to continue should be continually joined together.

44. Words, therefore, should always be taught and learned in combination with things, just as wine is bought and sold together with the cask that contains it, a dagger with its sheath, a tree with its bark, and fruit with its skin. For what are words but the husks and coverings of things? Therefore, when instruction is given in any language, even in the mother-tongue itself, the words must be explained by reference to the objects that they denote; and contrariwise, the scholars must be taught to express in language whatever they see, hear, handle, or taste,

so that their command of language, as it progresses, may ever run parallel to the growth of the understanding. The rule shall therefore run as follows:

The scholar should be trained to express everything that he sees in words, and should be taught the meaning of all the words that he uses. No one should be allowed to talk about anything without at the same time being able to express his knowledge in words. For he who cannot express the thoughts of his mind resembles a statue, and he who chatters, without understanding what he says, resembles a parrot. But we wish to train up men, and to do so with a minimum of labour, and this end can only be attained when instruction in language goes hand in hand with instruction in facts, and vice versa.

45. From this it follows that we ought to exclude from our schools all authors whose works merely teach words and do not at the same time lead to a knowledge of useful objects. We must bestow our labour on that which is of real importance, and, therefore (as Seneca says in his Ninth Letter), must devote ourselves to the improvement of our understanding rather than to the enlargement of our vocabulary. Anyone that wishes to read such books should skim through them out of school hours quickly and superficially without tedious explanations or attempts at imitation; since the time thus spent could be better employed in the study of more comprehensive books.

46. Exercises in reading and writing should always be combined. Even when scholars are learning their alphabet, they should be made to master the letters by writing them; since it is impossible to find a more agreeable method or one that will give them a greater incentive to work. For, since all children have a natural desire to draw, this exercise will give them pleasure, and the imagination will be excited by the twofold action of the senses. Later on, when they can read with ease, they should be made to exercise their powers on subject-matter that would in any case have to be learned, that is to say, something calculated to give them practical information or to instil morality or piety. The same plan may be adopted when they learn to read Latin, Greek, or Hebrew. It will be of great advantage to read and copy the declensions and conjugations over and over again, until, by this means, reading, writing, the meaning of the words, and the formation of the case-endings, have been thoroughly learned. In this case we have a fourfold result from a single exercise. A system of concentration that is of such vital importance should be applied to all branches of study, in order that, as Seneca says, what is learned

by reading may be given form by writing, or that, as St. Augustine says of himself, we may write while we make progress and make progress while we write.

47. As a rule, no care is shown in the choice of the subjects that are given as exercises in style, and there is no connexion between the successive subjects. The result is that they are exercises in style and nothing else, and have very little influence on the reasoning powers; indeed it frequently happens that, after much time and study have been devoted to them, they prove absolutely worthless and of no use for the business of life. Style should therefore be practised by means of the subject-matter of the particular science or art on which the reasoning powers of the class are being exercised. The teacher should tell his pupils stories about the originators of the subject and where and when they lived, or should give them exercises in imitation based on the subject-matter, so that, by a single effort, notions of style may be imbibed, the reasoning powers may be improved, and, since either the teacher or the pupils are continually talking, the faculty of speech also may be exercised.

48. Towards the end of the eighteenth chapter I have shown that it is possible for the scholars to give instruction in the subject that they have just learned, and, since this process not only makes them thorough but also enables them to make progress more rapidly, it should not be overlooked in this connexion.

49. Finally, it will be of immense use, if the amusements that are provided to relax the strain on the minds of the scholars be of such a kind as to lay stress on the more serious side of life, in order that a definite impression may be made on them even in their hours of recreation. For instance, they may be given tools, and allowed to imitate the different handicrafts, by playing at farming, at politics, at being soldiers or architects, etc. In spring they may be taken into the garden or into the country, and may be taught the various species of plants, vying with one another to see who can recognize the greater number. In this way they will be introduced to the rudiments of medicine, and not only will it be evident which of them has a natural bent towards botany, but in many the inclination will be created. Further, in order to encourage them, the mock titles of doctor, licentiate, or student of medicine may be given to those who make the greatest progress. The same plan may be adopted in other kinds of recreation. In the game of war the scholars may become field marshals, generals, captains, or standard bearers. In that of politics they may be kings, ministers, chancellors, secretaries, ambassadors, etc.,

and, on the same principle, councillors, provosts, lawyers, or officials; since such pleasantries often lead to serious things. Thus would be fulfilled Luther's wish that the studies of the young at school could be so organized that the scholars might take as much pleasure in them as in playing at ball all day, and thus for the first time would schools be a real prelude to practical life.

Seventh Problem

How are the subjects of study to be progressively graded?

50. How this can be done, we have seen in the Fourth, Sixth, Seventh and Eighth Principles of the sixteenth chapter, and in the Fifth, Sixth and Seventh Principles of the eighteenth chapter. The important point is that suitable books should be written for the classical schools, and that these should embody hints to the teacher for their proper use, so that learning, morality, and piety may be led from one stage to another until they reach the highest.

Eighth Problem

Of the removal and avoidance of obstructions.

51. Truly has it been said, that nothing is more useless than to learn and to know much, if such knowledge be of no avail for practical purposes; and again, that not he who knows much is wise, but he who knows what is useful. The task of schools will therefore be rendered easier if the subjects taught be curtailed. This can be done if omission be made:
(i)   Of all unnecessary matter.
(ii) Of all unsuitable matter.
(iii) Of all minute detail.

52. Anything is unnecessary that is productive neither of piety nor of morality and that is not essential for the cultivation of the mind. Such are the names of heathen deities, the myths connected with them, and the religious observances of the ancients, as well as the productions of scurrilous and indecent poets and dramatists. It may occasionally be

necessary for the individual to read these things in private, but in the schools, where the foundations of wisdom should be laid, nothing of the kind should be permitted. 'What madness it is', says Seneca, 'to learn so much trash, when time is so precious.' Nothing, therefore, should be learned solely for its value at school, but for its use in life, that the information which a scholar has acquired may not vanish as soon as he leaves school.

53. Knowledge is unsuitable when it is uncongenial to the mind of this or that scholar. For there is as great a difference between the minds of men as exists between the various kinds of plants, of trees, or of animals; one must be treated in one way, and another in another, and the same method cannot be applied to all alike. It is true that there are men of great mental power who can compass every subject; but there are also many who find the greatest difficulty in mastering the rudiments of some things. Some display great ability for abstract science, but have as little aptitude for practical studies as an ass has for playing on the lyre. Others can learn everything but music, while others again are unable to master mathematics, poetry, or logic. What should be done in these cases ? If we attempt to counteract a natural disinclination we are fighting against nature, and such effort is useless. For there will be either no result or one totally incommensurate with the energy expended. The teacher is the servant and not the lord of nature; his mission is to cultivate and not to transform, and therefore he should never attempt to force a scholar to study any subject if he see that it is uncongenial to his natural disposition; since it is more than probable that what is lacking in one direction will be compensated for in another. If one branch be cut off a tree, the others become stronger, because more vitality flows into them; and if none of the scholars be forced to study any subject against his will, we shall find no cases in which disgust is produced and the intelligence is blunted. Each one will develop in the direction of his natural inclinations (in accordance with the Divine will), and will serve God and man in his station in life, whatever that may be.

54. In the same way, if all minute and technical details (such as all the species of plants and of animals, all the various callings of mechanics, the names of all their tools and so forth) had to be learned, this would be a most wearisome and confusing task. In school work it is sufficient if the main classes that exist in nature, with their most important and most essential divisions (of course truthfully), be made thoroughly clear. More specialized knowledge can easily be acquired later, as the oppor-

tunity arises. Those who wish to win a speedy victory over the enemy, do not waste time in storming unimportant places, but go straight to the headquarters of the war; since it is certain that, if they can get the upper hand in a pitched battle, and capture the most important strongholds, all the others will surrender of their own accord. In the same way, if the principal points of any subject be mastered, the subsidiary details will be acquired with great ease. To this class of obstructions belong the voluminous dictionaries that contain every word in a language. For, since the greater number of them are never used, why should we force boys to learn them all, and thus overburden the memory?

So much for the saving of time and effort in teaching and in learning.

Chapter XX

The Method of the Sciences, specifically

We must now collect together the scattered observations that we have made on the proper teaching of the sciences, of the arts, of languages, of morality, and of piety. By proper teaching I mean teaching that combines ease, thoroughness, and rapidity.

2. Science, or the knowledge of nature, consists of an internal perception, and needs the same essentials as the external perception, namely the eye, an object, and light. If these be given, perception will follow. The eye of the inner perception is the mind or the understanding, the object is all that lies within or without our apprehension, while the light is the necessary attention. But, as in the case of external perception a definite procedure is necessary in order to apprehend things as they are, so with internal perception a certain method is necessary if things are

to be presented to the mind in such a way that it can grasp them and assimilate them with ease.

3. The youth who wishes to penetrate the mysteries of the sciences must carefully observe four rules:

(i) He must keep the eye of his mind pure.

(ii) He must see that the object be brought near to it.

(iii) He must pay attention.

(iv) He must proceed from one object to another in accordance with a suitable method. For thus he will apprehend everything surely and easily.

4. Over the amount of ability that we possess we have no control, for God has portioned out this mirror of the understanding, this inner eye, according to His will. But it lies in our power to prevent it from growing dusty or dim. By dust, I mean the idle, useless, and empty occupations of the mind. For our mind is in constant activity, like a continually running millstone, and is supplied by its servants, the external senses, with material from every side. But unless the overseer, the reason, be continually on the watch, worthless material is often supplied, such as chaff, straw, or sand, instead of corn or wheat. Thus it comes to pass that, as in the case of a mill, every corner is filled with dust. This inner mill, therefore, the mind (which is also a mirror) will be kept free from dust, if the young be kept away from worthless occupations and be skilfully trained to like worthy and useful things.

5. In order that the mirror may duly receive the images of the objects, it is necessary that these latter be solid and visible, and be also placed suitably before the eyes. Clouds and similar objects that possess little consistency make but a slight impression on a mirror, while objects that are not present make none at all. Those things, therefore, that are placed before the intelligence of the young, must be real things and not the shadow of things. I repeat, they must be things; and by the term I mean determinate, real, and useful things that can make an impression on the senses and on the imagination. But they can only make this impression when brought sufficiently near to the senses.

6. From this a golden rule for teachers may be derived. Everything should, as far as is possible, be placed before the senses. Everything visible should be brought before the organ of sight, everything audible before that of hearing. Odours should be placed before the sense of smell, and things that are tastable and tangible before the sense of taste and of touch respectively. If an object can make an impression on several

J.A. COMENII
DIDACTICA OPERA
OMNIA.
Ab Anno 1627 ad 1657.
continuata.

Frontispiece to *Didactica Omnia,* by Crispin de Pas.

senses at once, it should be brought into contact with several, though with the limitations imposed in the Eighth Principle of Chapter VIII.

7. For this there are three cogent reasons. Firstly, the commencement of knowledge must always come from the senses (for the understanding possesses nothing that it has not first derived from the senses). Surely, then, the beginning of knowledge should consist, not in the mere learning the names of things, but in the actual perception of the things themselves! It is when the thing has been grasped by the senses that language should fulfil its function of explaining it still further.

8. Secondly, the truth and certainty of science depend more on the witness of the senses than on anything else. For things impress themselves directly on the senses, but on the understanding only mediately and through the senses. This is evident from the fact that belief is at once accorded to knowledge derived from the senses, while an appeal is always made to them from *a priori* reasoning and from the testimony of others. We do not trust a conclusion derived from reasoning unless it can be verified by a display of examples (the trustworthiness of which depends on sensuous perception). No one could have such confidence in the testimony of another person as to disbelieve the experience of his own senses. Science, then, increases in certainty in proportion as it depends on sensuous perception. It follows, therefore, that if we wish to implant a true and certain knowledge of things in our pupils, we must take especial care that everything be learned by means of actual observation and sensuous perception.

9. Thirdly, since the senses are the most trusty servants of the memory, this method of sensuous perception, if universally applied, will lead to the permanent retention of knowledge that has once been acquired. For instance, if I have once tasted sugar, seen a camel, heard a nightingale sing, or been in Rome, and have on each occasion attentively impressed the fact on my memory, the incidents will remain fresh and permanent. We find, accordingly, that children can easily memorise Scriptural and secular stories from pictures. Indeed, he who has once seen a rhinoceros (even in a picture) or been present at a certain occurrence, can picture the animal to himself and retain the event in his memory with greater ease than if they had been described to him six hundred times. Hence the saying of Plautus: 'An eye-witness is worth more than ten ear-witnesses.' Horace also says: 'What is entrusted to the fickle ears makes less impression in the mind than things which are actually presented to the eyes and which the spectator stores up for himself.'

In the same manner, whoever has once seen a dissection of the human body, will understand and remember the relative position of its parts with far greater certainty than if he had read the most exhaustive treatises on anatomy, but had never actually seen a dissection performed. Hence the saying, 'Seeing is believing.'

10. If the objects themselves cannot be procured, representations of them may be used. Copies or models may by constructed for teaching purposes, and the same principle may be adopted by botanists, geometricians, zoologists, and geographers, who should illustrate their descriptions by engravings of the objects described. The same thing should be done in books on physics and elsewhere. For example, the human body will be well explained by ocular demonstration if the following plan be adopted. A skeleton should be procured (either such an one as is usually kept in universities, or one made of wood), and on this framework should be placed the muscles, sinews, nerves, veins, arteries, as well as the intestines, the lungs, the heart, the diaphragm, and the liver. These should be made of leather and stuffed with wool, and should be of the right size and in the right place, while on each organ should be written its name and its function. If you take the student of medicine to this construction and explain each part to him separately, he will grasp all the details without any effort, and from that time forth will understand this mechanism of his own body. For every branch of knowledge similar constructions (that is to say, images of things which cannot be procured in the original) should be made, and should be kept in the schools ready for use. It is true that expense and labour will be necessary to produce these models, but the result will amply reward the effort.

11. If any be uncertain if all things can be placed before the senses in this way, even things spiritual and things absent (things in heaven, or in hell, or beyond the sea), let him remember that all things have been harmoniously arranged by God in such a manner that the higher in the scale of existence can be represented by the lower, the absent by the present, and the invisible by the visible. This can be seen in the *Macromicrocosmus* of Robert Fludd, in which the origin of the winds, of rain, and of thunder is described in such a way that the reader can visualize it. Nor is there any doubt that even greater concreteness and ease of demonstration than is here displayed might be attained.

12. So much for the presentation of objects to the senses. We must now speak of the light, the absence of which renders the presentation of objects to the eyes useless. This light of the teaching art is attention, and

by its means the learner can keep his mind from wandering and can take in everything that is put before him. It is impossible for any man to see an object in the dark, or if his eyes be closed, no matter how near to him it may be; and in the same way, if you talk to one who is not attending, or show him anything, you will make no impression on his senses. This we can observe in the case of those who, while lost in thought, do not notice what is going on before their eyes. He, therefore, who wishes to show anything to another at night must provide light, and must polish the object so that it shines; and in the same way a master, if he wish to illumine with knowledge a pupil shrouded in the darkness of ignorance, must first excite his attention, that he may drink in information with a greedy mind. How this can be done we have shown in the Second Principle of the seventeenth chapter, and in the First Principle of the nineteenth chapter.

13. So much for the light. We will now speak of the mode in which objects must be presented to the senses, if the impression is to be distinct. This can be readily understood if we consider the processes of actual vision. If the object is to be clearly seen it is necessary: (1) that it be placed before the eyes; (2) not far off, but at a reasonable distance; (3) not on one side, but straight before the eyes; (4) and so that the front of the object be not turned away from, but directed towards, the observer; (5) that the eyes first take in the object as a whole; (6) and then proceed to distinguish the parts; (7) inspecting these in order from the beginning to the end; (8) that attention be paid to each and every part; (9) until they are all grasped by means of their essential attributes. If these requisites be properly observed, vision takes place successfully; but if one be neglected its success is only partial.

14. For instance, if any one wish to read a letter that has been sent him by a friend, it is necessary: (1) that it be presented to the eyes (for if it be not seen, how can it be read?);(2) that it be placed at a suitable distance from the eyes (for if it be too far off, the words cannot be distinguished); (3) that it be directly in front of the eyes (for if it be on one side, it will be confusedly seen); (4) that it be turned the right way up (for if a letter or a book be presented to the eyes upside down or on its side, it cannot be read); (5) the general characteristics of the letter, such as the address, the writer, and the date must be seen first (for unless these facts be known, the particular items of the letter cannot be properly understood); (6) then the remainder of the letter must be read, that nothing be omitted (otherwise the contents will not all be known, and

perhaps the most important point will be missed); (7) it must be read in the right order (if one sentence be read here and another there, the sense will be confused); (8) each sentence must be mastered before the next is commenced (for if the whole be read hurriedly, some useful point may easily escape the mind); (9) finally, when the whole has been carefully perused, the reader may proceed to distinguish between those points that are necessary and those that are superfluous.

15. These points should be observed by those who teach the sciences, and may be expressed in nine very useful precepts.

(i) Whatever is to be known must be taught.

Unless that which is to be known be placed before a pupil, how is he to acquire a knowledge of it? Therefore let those who teach beware of concealing anything from their pupils, whether of intent, as do the envious and dishonest, or through carelessness, as is the case with those who perform their duties in a perfunctory manner. The two things necessary are honesty and hard work.

16. (ii) Whatever is taught should be taught as being of practical application in everyday life and of some definite use.

That is to say, the pupil should understand that what he learns is not taken out of some Utopia or borrowed from Platonic ideas, but is one of the facts which surround us, and that a fitting acquaintance with it will be of great service in life. In this way, his energy and his accuracy will be increased.

17. (iii) Whatever is taught should be taught straightforwardly, and not in a complicated manner.

This means that we must look straight at objects and not squint, for in that case the eyes do not see that at which they look, but rather distort and confuse it. Objects should be placed before the eyes of the student in their true character, and not shrouded in words, metaphors, or hyperboles. These devices have their use if the object be to exaggerate or to detract from, to praise or to blame what is already known. But when knowledge is being acquired they should be avoided and the facts should be set forth plainly.

18. (iv) Whatever is taught must be taught with reference to its true nature and its origin; that is to say, through its causes.

This method of cognition is the best if the true nature of a fact is to be learned. For if its true nature be not made evident, this is not cognition but error. The true nature of a fact lies in the process that brought it into being. If it appear to contain elements not accounted for by that process, it is evident that there is some misapprehension. Now everything is brought into existence by its causes. Therefore to explain the causes of anything is equivalent to making a true exposition of that thing's nature, in accordance with the principles: 'Knowledge consists in having a firm grip of causes', and 'Causes are the guides of the understanding'. Objects can thus be best, easiest, and most certainly cognized through a knowledge of the processes that produced them. If a man wish to read a letter he holds it as it was written, inverted, or on its side, and in the same way, if a fact be explained by means of the process that gave it birth, it will be easily and surely understood. If, however, the teacher reverse the order of nature, he is certain to confuse the student. Therefore, the method employed in teaching should be based on the method of nature. That which precedes should be taken first, and that which follows, last.

19. (v) If anything is to be learned, its general principles must first be explained. Its details may then be considered, and not till then.

The reasons for this have been given in Chapter XVI, Principle 6. We give a general notion of an object when we explain it by means of its essential nature and its accidental qualities. The essential nature is unfolded by the questions, What? Of what kind? and Why? Under the question 'what' are included the name, the genus, the function, and the end. Under the question 'of what kind' comes the form of the object, or the mode in which it is fitted to its end. Under the question 'why' the efficient or causal force by which an object is made suitable to its end. For example, did I wish to give a student a general notion of a man, I should say: Man is (1) the chief creation of God, and destined for dominion over other creatures; (2) endowed with freedom of choice and action; (3) and on that account provided with the light of reason that he may direct his choice and his actions with wisdom. This is but a general notion of man, but it goes to the root of the matter and says everything about him that is essential. To these you may, if you like, add some of his accidental qualities, still keeping to generalities, and this must be done by asking the questions: From what origin? Whence? When? You may then proceed to his parts, the body and the soul. The nature of the body can be demonstrated through the anatomy of its organs; that of the soul by examining the faculties of which it consists. All these points must be taken in their proper order.

20. (vi) All the parts of an object, even the smallest, and without a single exception, must be learned with reference to their order, their position, and their connexion with one another.

Nothing exists in vain, and sometimes the strength of the larger parts depends on that of the smallest. Certain it is that in a clock, if one pin be broken or bent, or moved out of its place, the whole machine will stop. Similarly, in a living body, the loss of one organ may cause life to cease, and in a sentence it is often on the smallest words, such as prepositions and conjunctions, that the whole sense depends. Perfect knowledge of an object can therefore only be attained by acquiring a knowledge of the nature and function of each of its parts.

21. (vii) All things must be taught in due succession and not more than one thing should be taught at one time.

The organ of vision is unable to take in two or three objects at one time (certain it is that he who reads a book cannot look at two pages at once, nay, cannot even see two lines, though they lie quite close together, nor two words, nor two letters, otherwise than successively); and in the same way the mind can only grasp one thing at a time. We should therefore make a distinct break in our progress from one thing to another, that we may not overburden the mind.

22. (viii) We should not leave any subject until it is thoroughly understood.

Nothing can be done in a moment. For every process involves motion, and motion implies successive stages. The pupil should therefore not pass on from any point in a science until he has thoroughly mastered it and is conscious that he has done so. The methods to be employed are emphatic teaching, examination, and repetition, until the desired result is attained. This we have pointed out in Chapter XVIII, Principle 10.

23. (ix) Stress should be laid on the differences which exist between things, in order that what knowledge of them is acquired may be clear and distinct.

Much meaning lies concealed in that celebrated saying: 'He who distinguishes well is a good teacher.' For too many facts overwhelm a student, and too great a variety confuses him. Remedies must therefore be applied: in the first case, order, by means of which one thing may be taken after another; in the second, a careful consideration of differences, that it may always be evident in what respects one thing differs from another. This is the only method that can give distinct, clear, and certain knowledge; since the variety and actuality of objects depend on their distinctive attributes, as we have hinted in Chapter XVIII, Principle 6.

24. Now it is impossible that all teachers, when they enter on their profession, should be possessed of the requisite skill, and it is therefore

necessary that the sciences which are taught in schools be mapped out in accordance with the foregoing laws. If this be done it will be difficult for any teacher to miss his mark. For, if the laws be rigorously observed, it is beyond question that any man who is once admitted into the royal palace and is allotted a certain space of time can easily and without any trouble master its whole contents, its pictures, statues, carpets, and other ornaments; and just as easy will it be for a youth who is admitted to the theatre of this world to penetrate with his mental vision the secrets of nature, and from that time forward to move among the works of God and of man with his eyes opened.

Chapter XXI

The Method of the Arts

'Theory', says Vives, 'is easy and short, but has no result other than the gratification that it affords. Practice, on the other hand, is difficult and prolix, but is of immense utility.' Since this is so, we should diligently seek out a method by which the young may be easily led to put into practice what is laid down by the arts.

2. Art primarily requires three things: (1) A model or a conception; that is to say, an external form which the artist may examine and then try to imitate. (2) The material on which the new form is to be impressed. (3) The instruments by the aid of which the work is accomplished.

3. But when the instruments, the materials, and the model have been provided, three more things are necessary before we can learn an art: (1) a proper use of the materials; (2) skilled guidance; (3) frequent practice. That is to say, the pupil should be taught when and how to use his materials; he should be given assistance when using them that he may not make mistakes, or that he may be corrected if he do; and he should

not leave off making mistakes and being corrected until he can work correctly and quickly.

4. With respect to these points eleven canons must be observed: six on the use of materials; three on guidance; and two on practice.

5. What has to be done must be learned by practice.

Artisans do not detain their apprentices with theories, but set them to do practical work at an early stage; thus they learn to forge by forging, to carve by carving, to paint by painting, and to dance by dancing. In schools, therefore, let the students learn to write by writing, to talk by talking, to sing by singing, and to reason by reasoning. In this way schools will become workshops humming with work, and students whose efforts prove successful will experience the truth of the proverb: 'Our work makes us.'

6. A definite model of and rule for that which has to be made must always be provided.

This the student should first examine, and then imitate, as though he were following in the footsteps of a guide. For he who neither knows what has to be done nor how to do it, is unable to produce anything of himself, but must have a model placed before him. Indeed it is sheer cruelty to force anyone to do what you wish while he is ignorant what your wishes are; to demand, that is to say, that he form straight lines, right angles, or perfect circles, unless you first give him a ruler, a square, and a pair of compasses, and explain their use to him. Further, great care should be taken to provide in the schoolroom formulae for or models of everything that has to be made, and these, whether drawings and diagrams, or rules and models, should be correct, definite, and simple; easy both to understand and to imitate. There will then be no absurdity in demanding of a man that he see, when provided with a light; that he walk, when he already stands on his feet; or that he use the tools that are already in his hands.

7. The use of instruments should be shown in practice and not by words; that is to say, by example rather than by precept.

It is many years since Quintilian said: 'Through precepts the way is long and difficult, while through examples it is short and practicable.' But alas, how little heed the ordinary schools pay to this advice. The very beginners in grammar are so overwhelmed by precepts, rules, exceptions to the rules, and exceptions to the exceptions, that for the most part they do not know what they are doing, and are quite stupefied before they begin to understand anything. But we see that handicraftsmen do not proceed in this way. They do not begin by drumming rules into their apprentices. They take them into the workshop and bid them look at the work that has been produced, and then, when they wish to imitate this (for man is an imitative animal), they place tools in their hands and show them how they should be held and used. Then, if they make mistakes, they give them advice and correct them, often more by example than by mere words, and, as the facts show, the novices easily succeed in their imitation. For there is great truth in that saying of the Germans, 'A good leader finds a good follower.' Very apposite, too, is the remark of Terence, 'Do you go before; I will follow.' This is the way, namely, by imitating, and without any laborious rules, that children learn to walk, to run, to talk, and to play. Rules are like thorns to the understanding, and to grasp their meaning needs both attention and ability, while even the dullest students are aided by example. No one has ever mastered any language or art by precept alone; while by practice this is possible, even without precept.

8. Practice should commence with the rudiments and not with ambitious works.

A carpenter does not begin by teaching his apprentice to build turrets, but first shows him how to hold the axe, to cut down treess, to shape planks, to bore holes, and to fasten beams together. A painter does not make his pupil commence by painting portraits, but teaches him how to mix colours, to hold the brush, and to make lines; then to attempt rough outlines, and so on. He who teaches a boy how to read explains to him, not the contents of the book, but the names and nature of the letters, and shows him how they can be joined together into syllables; then he proceeds to words, and then to sentences. In the same way the beginner in grammar should learn, first how to inflect single words, then how to join two together. Then he may advance to one-member sentences, two- and three-member sentences till he reach complex sentences and finally continuous speech. So too in dialectic. The student should first learn to distinguish things and the concepts of things by means of their genera and species; then to classify them according to their mutual relationship (for such links exist between all things); then to define and distribute them; then to estimate the value of the things and their concepts in combination, seeking out the What, the Whence, and the Why, and whether it be necessary or contingent. When he has had sufficient practice in this, he may proceed to ratiocination and seek how to draw conclusions from given premises, and finally he may essay discursive reasoning or the complete conduct of disputations. The same course may with advantage be followed in rhetoric. The student should first devote some time to the collection of synonyms, and may then learn to add epithets to nouns, verbs, and adverbs. He may then proceed to the use of antithesis, and later on to that of periphrasis. Then he may substitute figurative words for the originals, alter the order of the words for the sake of euphony, and adorn a simple sentence with all the figures of speech. Finally, when thoroughly versed in all these several points, and not sooner, he may proceed to the composition of a complete discourse. If anyone advance step by step in any art, as here indicated, it is impossible that he should not make rapid and solid progress.

The basis of the foregoing was discussed in Chapter XVII, Principle 4.

9. Beginners should at first practise on a material that is familiar to them.

This rule we obtain from the Ninth Principle of the seventeenth chapter, and from the Sixth Corollary of the Fourth Principle. Its meaning is that students should not be overburdened with matters that are unsuitable to their age, comprehension, and present condition, since otherwise they will spend their time in wrestling with shadows. For example, when a Polish boy is learning to read or to write his letters he should not be taught to do so from a book written in Latin, Greek, or Arabic, but from one written in his own language, that he may understand what he is doing. Again, if a boy is to understand the use of the rules of dialectic, the examples on which he is made to practise them should not be taken from Virgil or from Cicero, or from theological, political or medical writers, but should refer to the objects that surround him, to his books, to his clothes, to trees, houses, and schools. It will also be of use if the examples that are taken to illustrate the first rule be retained, although familiar, to illustrate the remainder. In dialectic, for example, a tree may be taken, and its genus, its species, its relations to other objects, its characteristic peculiarities and the logical definition and distribution of the term may be treated of. We may then proceed to the various ways in which a statement may be made about a tree. Finally, we may show how, by a perfect train of reasoning, and by taking the facts already ascertained as our starting-point, we may discover and demonstrate other properties of a tree. In this way, if, in each case, the use of the rules be illustrated by the same familiar example, the boy will easily master their application to all other subjects.

10. At first the prescribed form should be imitated with exactness. Later on more freedom may be allowed.

A form will be expressed with more exactness in proportion as care is taken to make it resemble its original. Thus coins that are struck by one die are exactly like the dies and one another. So also with books printed from metal type, and with casts made in wax, plaster, or metal. In all other artistic operations, therefore, as far as is possible, any imitation (at any rate the first) should be an exact copy of its original, until the hand, the mind, and the tongue gain more confidence, and can produce good imitations by working freely on their own lines. For instance, those who learn writing take a thin and transparent sheet of paper, place it over the copy that they wish to imitate, and thus can easily form the letters that show through. Or the characters may be printed very faintly in a yellow or brownish colour on a white page, so that the pupil may go over them with pen and ink, and in this way may easily acquire the habit of shaping them. The same thing holds good in style, for each construction, sentence or period from a classic author set, another should be composed to resemble the original. If the original phrase be 'Rich in possessions', the boy should be made to imitate it by saying, 'Rich in coins', 'Rich in moneys', 'Rich in flocks', 'Rich in vineyards'. When Cicero says, 'In the opinion of the most learned men, Eudemus easily holds the first place in astrology', this may be copied with very little alteration as 'In the opinion of the greatest orators, Cicero easily holds the first place in eloquence'. 'In the opinion of the whole Church, St. Paul easily holds the first place in Apostleship.' So too in logic, if the well-known dilemma be given: It is either day or night. But it is night; therefore it is not day; the boy may learn to imitate it by similarly opposing contradictory conceptions to one another. As, 'He is either unlearned or learned. But he is unlearned; therefore he is not learned'; 'Cain was either pious or impious but he was not pious'; and so on.

11. The models of the objects that have to be produced must be as perfect as is possible, so that if any exercise himself sufficiently in imitating them it will be possible for him to become perfect in his art.

It is impossible to draw straight lines with a curved ruler, and in the same way a good copy cannot be made from a bad model. Great care should therefore be taken that models be prepared of everything that is to be done in school, or indeed in life, and that these be exact, simple, and easy to imitate. They may be either models, pictures and drawings, or precepts and rules; but the last-named must be very short, very clear, self-evident, and absolutely correct.

12. The first attempt at imitation should be as accurate as possible, that not the smallest deviation from the model be made.

That is to say, as far as is possible. For whatever comes first is, as it were, the foundation of that which follows. If the foundation be firm, a solid edifice can be constructed upon it, but if it be weak this is impossible. According to the observations of physicians, the initial defects of digestion cannot be repaired later on, and similarly in any operation an error at the beginning vitiates all that follows. For this reason Timotheus the musician used to demand twice as large a fee from those pupils who had learned the rudiments of their art elsewhere, saying that his labour was twofold, as he had first to get them out of the bad habits that they had acquired, and then to teach them correctly. Those, therefore, who are learning any art should take care to make themselves masters of the rudiments by imitating their copies accurately. This difficulty once overcome, the rest follows of itself, just as a city lies at the mercy of foes when its gates are broken in. All haste should be avoided, lest we proceed to advanced work before the elementary stages have been mastered. He goes fast enough who never quits the road, and a delay which is caused by obtaining a thorough grip of first principles is really no delay, but a great economy so as to master what follows with ease, speed, and accuracy.

13. Errors must be corrected by the master on the spot; but precepts, that is to say the rules, and the exceptions to the rules, must be given at the same time.

Hitherto we have urged that the arts be taught rather by example than by precept: we now add that precepts and rules must be given as well, that they may guide the operations and prevent error. That is to say, the less obvious points of the model should be clearly explained, and it should be made evident how the operation should begin, what it should aim at, and how that aim can be realized. Reasons should also be given for each rule. In this way a thorough knowledge of the art, and confidence and exactness in imitating, will be attained.

But these rules should be as short and as simple as possible, since we do not want to grow grey while acquiring them. When once mastered they should be of perpetual use, even when laid aside, just as knee-bands are of use to a child who is learning to walk, and, though they are afterwards discarded, the advantage derived from them remains.

14. The perfect teaching of art is based on synthesis and analysis.

We have already shown (Chapter XVIII, Principle 5) by examples taken from nature and the workshop that in this relation synthesis is

FILMSTRIP ON COMENIUS
AS AN EDUCATOR

In 1657, publication was first begun in the Netherlands of the complete works of John Amos Comenius, the great Moravian educator. In commemoration of the third centenary of this event, Unesco is producing a filmstrip depecting various stages in his life and highlighting the importance of his work. Photographs taken from Comenius's illustrated works and recent iconographic documents, draw particular attention to his rôle as a pioneer in education.

The filmstrip emphasizes the part played by Comenius as a precursor of audio-visual education, the importance of which he had already stressed in the 17th Century.

The filmstrip shows the revolutionary character of Comenius's work in his own day and underlines the growing importance of audio-visual techniques in present-day education. The filmstrip is intended for the general public, teachers and all those who are interested in educational questions.

For information concerning the availability of the filmstrip and its accompanying commentary, please write to:

> *Visual Media Division*
> *Department of Mass Communication*
> *Unesco, 19 Avenue Kléber, Paris 16⁰, France*

more important. The following points in addition will show that synthetic exercises should generally come first: (1) We should always commence with what is easy, and our own efforts are easier to understand than those of other people. (2) Writers take pains to conceal the artifices by which their results are obtained, so that at first the student finds difficulty in understanding what he sees, or fails to do so altogether. This difficulty would be removed if he began by practising on his own attempts, which are void of artifice. (3) The chief thing aimed at should be given the chief place in practice, and our real aim is to accustom the student of art to produce original work, and not merely to copy what is placed before him (see Chapter XVIII, Principle 5).

15. For all this, the accurate analysis of the work of others must not be neglected. It is only by continually traversing it that we get to know a road, its by-paths, and its crossroads. Besides, the variety that exists in nature is so great that it is impossible for rules to cover it or for one mind to master it. Many processes require many rules to express them, and these we can only learn if we analyse and study, and by imitation and emulation put ourselves in a position to produce similar results.

16. It is our wish then that in each art complete and exact models or patterns of everything that can be produced in that art be supplied to the student. Marginal precepts also and rules should be given him to help him to carry out the processes, to guide his efforts at imitation, to show him how to avoid making faults, and to correct them when made. Then other and different models should be given him, and these he should learn to classify and compare with the models that he has already used, and by copying a model that is like one previously used to produce works that resemble the original. After this, the finished works of other artists (who must be well known) may be examined and analysed in accordance with the models and rules that are already familiar. In this way the student will learn to employ the rules with greater ease, and will acquire the art of concealing his art. Only after a course of exercises of this kind will he be in the position to criticise artistic productions, whether his own or those of others.

17. These exercises must be continued until artistic production becomes second nature.

For it is practice, and nothing else, that produces an artist.

[Translated from the Latin by M. W. Keatinge (Didactica Omnia, A. & C. Black, London, 1896), revised by Mrs. Iris Urwin.]

The Pampaedia

The Pampaedia is the fourth part of the *General Consultation on the Reform of Human Affairs,* which is in seven parts and was planned in outline by Comenius at the end of the Thirty Years' War. The author desired to help strengthen peace, once it was restored, by means of a system of 'pansophic' philosophy accompanied by concrete proposals regarding the organization of learning, educational institutions, and religious and political life. *The Pampaedia* was begun after 1650, and most of it was written during Comenius' stay in Amsterdam. It remained in manuscript, like the greater part of the *Consultation,* the bulk of which—including *The Pampaedia*—was long thought to have been lost and was rediscovered only at the beginning of the second world war by D. Cyževskij in the archives of the Francke Orphanage at Halle. *The Pampaedia* was issued in Czech, by J. Hendrich, in 1948; the original Latin has not yet been published.

The educational scheme it contains is wider in scope than that of *The Great Didactic,* though some of its sections are more 'diagrammatic'. It is not confined to the school age proper, but embraces the entire course of human life. Education begins in the womb, and never comes to an end. Self-instruction supplements regular education, but the background of the whole conception is the philosophic idea that the whole world is a school for mankind.

The Pampaedia may be outlined as follows: (a) explanation of the subject and of the aims pursued; (b) proof that a plan for the general education of all is necessary, possible and easy to implement; (c) enumeration of the resulting requirements in respect of schools, new textbooks, and teachers; (d) review of the different 'schools' which man attends during the various stages of his existence (birth, infancy, childhood, adolescence, youth, adulthood, old age); (e) discussion of the advantages of the system.

95

The passages quoted comprise the first five chapters of the work; these start with the general idea of 'absolutely universal' education, and lead up to the school system which such an idea would produce.

Photocopy of a manuscript page by J. A. Comenius.

Chapter I

What universal education is and why
it is to be desired, 1-10 ; in what sense we want learning for all men,
about all things and in all ways, 11-15.

Pampaedia is universal education for the whole of the human race; for among the Greeks πάιδεία means both teaching itself and the discipline by which men acquire education, while πᾶν means universal. Therefore our goal is to be: learning πάντες, πάντα, πάντως (for all men, about all things, in all ways).

2. Let this desire for universal education remind us of what is to be considered under the prime classification, which we have seen in the realm of ideas: *Nothing, Something, Everything,* in order better to clarify our desire and the measure of our desire.

3. *Nothing* is here *no education at all,* such as we see with pity and horror among the most barbarous peoples, where unhappy mortals are born, live and die after the manner of beasts.

4. *Something* is here *some degree of education,* to this or that end, such as can be seen among more cultivated peoples who share among themselves the sciences, the arts, languages and other knowledge.

5. *Everything* will here be *universal education,* by which we seek to give man, the image of God, whatever is possible for the greatest glory he can attain beneath Heaven.

6. This desire resolves into three parts. Our first wish is that all men should be educated fully to full humanity; not any one individual, nor a few nor even many, but all men together and singly, young and old, rich and poor, of high and of lowly birth, men and women—in a word, all whose fate it is to be born human beings: so that at last the whole of the human race may become educated, men of all ages, all conditions, both sexes and all nations.

7. Our second wish is that every man should be wholly educated, rightly formed not only in one single matter or in a few or even in many, but in all things which perfect human nature; that he should be able to know the truth and not be deluded by what is false; to love good and

not be seduced by evil; to do what should be done and not permit what should be avoided; to talk wisely about everything with everybody when there is need, and not to be dumb in any matter; and finally to deal with things, with men and with God in all matters reasonably and not hastily, thereby never wandering from the goal of happiness.

8. And educated in all ways. Not to pomp and show, but to truth; that is to say, in order to make men as like as possible to the image of God, in which they were created: truly rational and wise, truly active and spirited, truly moral and honourable, truly pious and holy; and thereby truly happy and blessed, both here and in eternity.

9. Briefly: in order to enlighten all men with true wisdom; to order their lives by true government; to unite them with God by true religion so that none may mistake his mission in this world. This can be achieved if all learn:

(i) To be ignorant of nothing that is necessary, looking at all things with open eyes;

(ii) Choosing what is best and acting calmly in all situations, to delight in all things but need little;

(iii) Finding the highest good and uniting indissolubly with that alone, to achieve blessedness.

In a word: to be wise for eternity, but not to be unwise here.

10. Therefore we propose to recommend three unusual things, repeating ourselves in order to be clearly understood: that we should set out to lead towards universal education (1) all men (2) in all things, so that they become educated (3) in all ways.

11. All men: that is to say, all peoples, conditions, families, persons, never omitting anybody; for all are human beings with the same future life before them and the same road leading to it, pointed out by God but beset with snares and divers obstacles. It will therefore be necessary to warn and instruct all men prudently about these things, in order to drive foolishness from out our midst, if that be possible, so that the lament of wise men that 'the world is full of fools' will be no longer called for.

12. In all things: that is to say, in all things that can make man wise and happy. But what are these things? They are the four wise things which Solomon commends in the four exceeding wise little creatures:

(i) Provision for the future, which he praises in the ants (Proverbs, xxx. 25);

(ii) Prudence in the present, to do nothing except by safe ways, which he observes in the conies (v. 26);

(iii) Inclination to concord, without coercive force, which he praises in the locusts (v. 27);

(iv) Finally, that whatever is done, however slight, should be harmonious, regular and systematic; as is the work of the spider, even if otherwise it is useless (v. 28).

This then is what we seek by the universal education of the mind: that all men (1) should be equipped with knowledge for their future life and filled with longing for it, and led along the right paths to it; (2) should be taught so to enclose the business of this life in the bounds of prudence that all things here are secure to the best possible degree; (3) should learn so to walk in the paths of concord that none may go dangerously astray on the road of time and eternity and that they may restore dissidents to unity; and finally (4) should be filled with such ardour in their thoughts, words and deeds that all three may be as much in harmony as is possible. Achieving these four things, unhappy mortals would have an antidote for their unhappiness; most of them take no thought for the future, hazard the present, each disagreeing with all the rest and with himself (in thoughts, words and deeds), struggling and wasting themselves in discord and perishing.

13. In all ways: that is to say, towards truth, so that rightly formed by her each man will stand beyond the precipices of error and hazard, and walk in the paths of righteousness. For now few mortals rely on their own foundation or that of things; most of them follow blind instinct, or the opinions of others. These disagreeing diversely with each other and with things themselves, there is no end to hesitation, stumbling, lapsing and finally ruin. If an equal remedy is to be sought for this evil, it cannot be other than to follow not the guidance of blind habit or persuasion, but the adamantine rule of God and of things themselves, and for every man through all this to learn, to know and to be able to stand firmly everywhere and to walk everywhere in safety.

14. May I repeat our desire for the third time? Allow this, I beg, so that what we would strive for may be clear in all ways. We want all men to become pansophists, i.e.:

(i) Understanding the articulation of things, thoughts and words;

(ii) Understanding the aims, means and manner of carrying out all actions (their own and those of other people);

(iii) Able to distinguish the essential from the accidental, the indifferent from the dangerous, in actions diverging from and converging on the goal (and similarly in thoughts and words). And hence able to observe digression of thoughts, words and deeds, both their own and others, and at all times and in all places to know how to turn them back to the right path—

For if all men were to learn all things in all ways, all men would be wise and the world would be full of order, light and peace.

15. Bearing this in mind, we can already define universal education differently, and more precisely: it is a levelled road for spreading the light of pansophy over the minds, words and deeds of men. Or a means by which wisdom can be transplanted in the minds, tongues, hearts and hands of all men. For this reason we have placed on the frontispiece of this treatise a symbol taken from the gardener's craft: there gardeners are taking shoots from the tree of all knowledge and grafting them on to young trees, anxious to fill the whole of God's garden, our human race, with young trees of a like nature.

Chapter II

To what degree it is needful (1-14), possible (15-20), and easy (21-30), to educate all men to humanity.

It would be superfluous to trouble ourselves at length about this matter, if there were more men like Moses, desiring all the people to be prophets, than like Joshua. But since my wish, so like to that of Moses, became known, I have found so many opponents, that I cannot keep silent. For they have come not only from among open enemies (who have prime interest to rule in darkness and keep all the people in ignorance)—they have made up their minds to censure my proposal publicly, clamouring for steps to be taken against such temerity, whence new and dangerous heresies might arise: but even among friends of mine and of Truth are those who whisper in my ear (as once did Peter to his Christ) 'Be it far from thee!' You will expose yourself to ridicule! You will see all conditions of men confounded. Who will remain at the plough? And so on.

2. And so I feel the necessity is laid upon me to demonstrate as clearly as the sun shines in the heavens, this triune truth.

(i) As fervently as we love God (whose glory has the right to see His image before him as glorious as possible), and as sincerely as we cherish Christ (whose kingdom is the kingdom of light), and finally as truly as we hold dear the human race (the greater part of which is still engulfed in darkness), so truly, sincerely and deeply must we desire to drive darkness away from everywhere and that light should shine more brightly in all minds.

(ii) There is no lack of sufficient means to attain this desire.

(iii) There will be no lack of easy ways of putting this holy wish into effect, if industry is not lacking.

3. The need to educate all men becomes apparent if we consider that it is in the interests of God, of men and of things themselves. Of God, that He may not be frustrated in His ends through man; of men, that they may not lose the consort of God, that is to say their own beatitude; of things, that they need not for ever be subject to vanity, when men use them improperly (that is to say, neither for the glory of God nor for their own salvation). Let us consider these things more closely one by one.

4. It is to be desired that God should achieve His aim in creating man. I mean that aim which God Himself, conceiving the notion of creating man, expressed in these words: 'Let us make man in our image, after our likeness, and let them have dominion over the . . . cattle and over all the earth' (Genesis, I. 26). And when He said to him He had created: 'Subdue the earth and have dominion over it' (v. 28), whence it is clear that God created this rational creature, Man, primarily in order to have His image without Himself, in which to delight. In the second place, for the inferior creatures to have a guardian. And thirdly, for that same Man to rule, that is to say, for him to be his own arbiter, with the knowledge and ability to govern himself as well. All is to be glory of the wisdom of God, who ordains all things so wisely. (Proverbs, XVI. 4). Whence it follows that if any man lose his likeness to God (that is to say, loses the knowledge and ability to delight his Creator, to rule His creatures, and to govern his own self), by this he wanders from his Creator's goal and instead of God's glory ignominy results. To prevent this, and to prevent

God being frustrated in His ends through man, and robbed of His glory, is to be desired and to be earnestly sought.

5. It is in the interests of man that no one who partakes of human nature should stray from the purpose for which he was brought into the world. For it is vain to go and not to arrive; to follow and not to overtake; to seek and not to find; to do and not to accomplish; to desire and not to achieve. What profit it a man to be in the world and not to know, do and achieve that for which he was brought into the world? It were better not to be born. Therefore since all men are born, we must ensure that no one should later regret having been born. How is this to be done?

6. In the first place, we must see to it that no man lives as the beasts, but according to the dictates of reason, whose light is given to all; but not all know how to make use of that which is given to all, unless they are taught. Therefore they must be taught. Otherwise it will be such foolishness as to have fields which you do not till, to have a musical instrument you do not play, to have eyes you do not see with, to have ears you do not listen with, to have feet you do not walk with, and so on. For what would be the good of a reasonable nature not taught to use reason? Why should we want some men to be blessed with gifts of the spirit in vain (and all are blessed)? It is a different matter if lands lie fallow which are empty of inhabitants, for there is no one to till them, because there is no one to need them. The earth whether it is cultivated or neglected is a transitory thing, a thing only of this life. The human soul is a thing of eternity, and cannot be neglected without eternal loss (casting aside human salvation and injuring the glory of God).

7. It is to be desired not only that men should not live as beasts, but that they should become as wise as possible. For we are all made in the image of the most wise God, wherefore we must strive to make the copy true to the model. And since 'the multitude of the wise is the welfare of the world' (Wisdom, VI. 24), we cannot hope for full salvation unless it can be brought about that just as now 'the world is full of fools', so later the world will be full of wise men; wherefore let all men act rightly and none corrupt.

8. In the third place, since it is to be desired that no man should degenerate into not being a man, it is therefore to be desired that no man should remain without education; for through the force of human nature itself it is very easy for those who are devoid of education to degenerate so. For the mind's power of cognition, if not occupied with proper objects to direct it, creates for itself all kinds of vain-imaginings to

deceive it, however monstrous they may be. The power of will, if it is not directed to what is indeed right and good and would provide healthy pleasure, seizes on whatever is false, rejoices in harmful instead of useful things, destroying itself. Finally the power of action, if it is not directed in the way it should go, undertakes unsuitable affairs and either wears itself out to no good or else in addition brings harm to itself and others. It is certainly desirable that this should not happen.

9. And since the only cause of so many lapses everywhere is blindness of the mind, for which men do not know either their own ends or those of things, or legitimate ways of using them, it is absolutely essential for all men (whom we have to warn of constant eternal abysses) to be rightly informed about all these things. For it is certain that whenever mortals sin in thought, will or deed, there is always one root of transgression—that they take no care for the ends, means and ways; particularly the ultimate ends, to which all should tend in everything (and most particularly in man himself). For if the principal goal is ignored, then it is very easy to be led away by incidental trifles and to fall away from the true ends in favour of the false. It is certainly harmful for this to happen in any matter; but it is infinitely worse if man himself takes no care for his end and wanders from it; in the first case he destroys other things, but in the second he destroys himself. Nought so effective in limiting (or at least in lessening) extravagances throughout the human race could therefore be imagined than that all men should begin to consider why they are here and for what purpose each single thing is here with them, and that they should then begin to understand and to ordain their actions accordingly.

10. It is also to be desired that even utterly barbarous peoples should be enlightened and liberated from the shades of their barbarity, for they are a part of the human race and the part should be like the whole; and further, the whole is not whole if any part is lacking. Finally, to prefer the part to the whole (in the possession of anything good) is clear proof of lack of right judgement or of good will. Whoever then does not wish to show something of foolishness or ill will, must wish good to all men, and not only to himself, a few of his own near ones, or his own nation. For it cannot even go well with the whole body if it does not go well with all its members together and singly; for they are so bound together that if any one of them, even the smallest, is affected, it is immediately felt by them all, and one sick limb easily affects another. Nor is it otherwise in human society; for one man is infected by another man, one city

by another city, one nation by another nation: but if all were healthy they would enjoy their common weal together. He then who would seriously not wish well to the whole of the human race, injures the whole human race. Nor is he a true friend to his own person if he wishes the healthy to mix with the sick, the wise man with fools, the good man with evil men, the fortunate man with unfortunates; yet this cannot be avoided if he indeed wishes only himself, and not others, to be whole, wise, good and happy.

11. In a word: where God has made no distinctions, it is undesirable for any man to make them; lest we should want to seem wiser than God Himself, ordering things otherwise than as He has done. But God made no distinctions between men, in respect of that which constitutes human nature; for He made all (1) of one blood (Acts, XVII. 26)—behold, one material! (2) partakers of the same divine image (Genesis I. 26)—behold, one form! (3) models from the hands of the same artist (ibid.)—behold, one origin! (4) inheritors of the same eternity (Matthew, XXV. 34)—behold, one end! (5) We are all sent into the same school of the world and charged with preparing ourselves for another life. Behold, all is one! Why then are we not all admitted to all things which would fit us for all things? It is lamentable, utterly unjust and insulting that while all men are admitted to God's theatre, all are not given the chance of looking at everything! While all are invited to Heaven, all are not taught the way to reach Heaven! While all daily observe the things created for all men, most of them, like the beasts which are devoid of reason, do not know what those things are or for what purpose they exist and come into being.

12. But not even in those things which accede and are attribute to human nature from without did God wish to have too great differences between us; for it to be clear that the same remedies are needed to meet the same cases. All have the same lot in birth and death, but in between we seem to see differences; yet even here there is a similarity in the vicissitudes we are subject to. The common people, the farmers, the beggars and the barbarians all have their losses and their lots; kings and princes and philosophers have theirs. For all alike time passes by in pleasant expectation, but in painful reality, unless we know the remedy for our troubles. That cannot come from elsewhere than the pursuit of true wisdom. If any man thinks that he or his do not need this pursuit, he is withdrawing himself and his people from the common lot of humanity, hurtling unarmed against so many temporal and eternal des-

tinies; he would be acting with temerity, and forcing others to like temerity with him. How unhappy the man who does not know the wondrous happiness he has lost, nor the misery of the misfortune into which he has fallen, nor the way to flee the latter or to repair the former !

13. Finally it is in the interests of things themselves for all men to be trained for a rational life, for the latter too are better off under the wise government of the wise. For just as a garden is better off under a good gardener, craft under a good craftsman, a family under a wise husband-man, a kingdom under a wise king, an army under an experienced leader, than under a bad one: so too things are better off under men who own them and make use of their rights, knowing how to use them aright. What Solomon says is worthy of note: 'A righteous man regardeth the life of his beast, but the tender mercies of the wicked are cruel' (Proverbs, XII. 10). What cruelty do all things suffer everywhere, when through the wickedness and ignorance of man they are used for wrong purposes ! The Apostle hints at this, when he testifies that all creatures are made subject to vanity, sighing and longing, yea hoping for liberation from the bondage of such evil servitude (Romans, VIII. 20). Surely it is to be desired that this wish and hope of all creation should be fulfilled, that things should go better for everything everywhere, and that all creatures should have cause to praise the Lord with us (Psalm 148). It is therefore also to be desired that all men should be taught to know and understand things properly, and to use and enjoy them rightly; this has nowhere happened nor can it happen, without education of the mind.

14. Thus the necessity for universal education (with regard to God, men and things) is clear. But someone may say: Such high hopes are vain if that which is desired is of things which are impossible. I agree, if that is the case: but I deny that it is so. For it is not possible that God would ordain a goal for all things without providing the means to that goal, if He is wise. Let us consider it from this point of view too: we shall see that all men are endowed with everything that can educate them for humanity. For:

15. One of the means through which man can reach his goal is man himself; he is so made that he can achieve perfection if he so desires; and he does so desire and is capable, if he is rightly informed in the matter. But if he does not so desire, the fault lies with him: his Creator can then indeed say: 'I would have, and ye would not !' (Matthew, XXIII. 37). Thus if Adam had been content with his position (subject to his Creator) he would have remained the image of God, pure, holy, wise, governing

things and himself, and (as the Scriptures say) the glory of God (1 Corinthians, XI. 7). But since he broke away, not God, but man became
powerless; yet if he abide not in unbelief and contumacy, God is able
to graft him in again (Romans, XI. 23). Therefore just as all other things
were provided with the organs required for the purpose for which they
were created, and just as the proper analysis of their structure reveals
their ends: so Man, if he is properly observed in all his parts and shown
unto himself, can see in himself his divine and sublime goal and can order
his affairs in accordance with it, as we have seen in the sections on
Pansophy.

16. Moreover, human nature, being entirely active, pours itself out
completely wherever it turns; it is therefore very suitable for education.
This is clear; for human nature is part of the common Nature, which
cannot be inactive, as can be proved by induction from all natural activity.
Water flows down a slope in whatever direction you provide an opening;
if you give none, it finds one for itself and causes a flood. The sun's rays
will be reflected by a mirror wherever you wish; if you hold up no mirror,
the rays either fall on the water and are reflected abroad, or throw their
light over the ground, woods, buildings, sky, etc. And so it is in all
things.

17. Nor is there any lack of aids given to all by Heaven, for all things
that make man wise have been given to all: both the Books of God, and
the organs with which to read the Books of God—the senses, the reason,
and faith. Nobody doubts the book of the world, for all see it opening
daily for all to see. Nor does anyone doubt the book of the mind, in
which all read night and day, and each man singly whether wise or fool-
ish. But it would be possible to doubt the book of the revelations contained in the Holy Scriptures; for not all possess it, nor do all who have
it read it; and there are many who do not even know that such a book
exists. Yet we have God's commandment that none shall be kept far
from it (not even the children, Deuteronomy, XXXI. 12); they that read
in this book and meditate thereon day and night are praised (Psalm 1, 2;
Acts, XVII. 11), and that from very childhood (2 Timothy, III. 15); finally
all people are exhorted to hear what the Lord says (Psalm 49, 1 and elsewhere). It cannot be doubted that the Lord wishes this book, too, to be
common to all men, at least now when the world is drawing to an end.
Although for a time He withdrew His law from the peoples on account
of their idolatry (and therefore their desertion of themselves), after reconciliation with the world through Christ He commanded them to go

into all the world and preach the mystery of salvation to every creature (Mark, XVII. 5), prophesying in all the world (Matthew, XXIV. 14) that 'the earth shall be full of the knowledge of the Lord, as the waters cover the sea' (Isaiah, XI. 9). Wherefore let this book, at least now, at the end of the ages, be made common to all, and let all be taught to use all the books of God for all to be able to draw wisdom from them, especially when there is no doubt about their organs. For all are endowed with senses with which to perceive all that is in the world, and reason with which to examine all the consequences of what human wisdom does, and faith by which to admit all that trustworthy witnesses report, etc. Thus all is sufficiently provided for.

18. The instruments of education are given not only to all in any one nation, but to everybody all over the world. By this I mean all the senses both external and internal, together with the objects of the senses; and the mind, fully equipped with common knowledge, instincts and faculties; and the heart, the seat of the affections and longing for the highest good; and similarly the tongue, for the mutual communication of all things; the hands, for the similar performance of all similar things; and the late time of growing up, sufficient to achieve all things, etc. Nowhere among the peoples is it otherwise.

19. Not only are all these things given to all peoples, but to all men singly of all peoples, through the identity of human nature everywhere. For the internal structure of all men is as one as is their bodily structure. Whatever one man is by nature, has, wishes, knows or is able, the same are, have, wish, know and are able all the rest. Truly can we say with the poet: 'If you know one you know all'. Whoever reads these words, let him judge the whole of the human race by his own self. Whatever you feel you wish, know and perceive, the same may anyone else feel he perceives, knows, wishes; for he is equipped with the same organs. Therefore if all were led in the same paths it would not be possible but that all should be brought to the same goal. There is no difference at all in this matter, though there may be many differences in degree; one may comprehend more quickly than another, respond more eagerly, or remember more tenaciously. But livelier or slower mind, judgement or memory does not decide whether you are a man or not; but only whether you proceed more quickly or more slowly. If any man say: 'We are corrupt', I shall answer: (1) We are restored through the new Adam. (2) We have been commanded to put right what is corrupt, to break up the fallow ground and sow not among thorns (Jeremiah, IV. 3), which is

the purpose of the whole education of the mind. If you say: 'Some men are slow', I shall answer: No man is entirely wooden, and those of slower mind are often stronger in body; they are therefore more suited to endure toil and should not be left without help.

20. Finally, why should it not be possible to teach men to use things rightly and not abuse them, if they are taught that it goes well with things if each is in the state proper to it and so administered that it can usefully offer that which it should? For Pansophy teaches us (and all men can learn it there) that there is nought in heaven or earth, in the water or the air or anywhere else, that was not destined for human use, either directly or indirectly; this is clear from the world of nature. And from the world of human labour it is clear that nothing serves its rightful purpose unless it is rightly used, and that things themselves cannot use themselves rightly, but must be used by man. If all are taught to observe this truth, the world can be rid of so much dreadful and abominable abuse.

21. It is therefore clear that it is no impossible recommendation to suggest that all men without exception should be educated for humanity. Yet since it is not sufficient for a thing to be possible, for men also seek facility in what is to be done, considering that which is difficult to be impossible, nor understanding the words: 'Manly courage strains towards the heights', we must make it quite clear that we are not asking for anything to be undertaken that is not as prompt and easy as it is desirable and possible through human nature itself, provided we know how rightly to use the means provided by God, and wish to use them. Let us consider this assertion in the guise of a few more or less mechanical problems.

Problem I

22. *To direct everything with regard to its own goal, including man.*
No art is required for this, provided the impediments which stand in the way of natural inclination are removed; e.g., there is no need to force round things to move, square things to stay still, heavy things to fall, etc.; they hurry of their own accord once obstacles are removed. Therefore drive away from man's intellect the darkness which makes him brutish, so that being truly aware of his sublime nature he may realize that he must strive to be above all things (that is to say, have

dominion over things, govern himself by himself, and gloriously come nearer to the likeness of God); you will see that he is by nature more than sufficiently ambitious in these things. Experience will show that there is no need of force, but that wise and holy guidance is all that is required. For there is no man, no man at all, who holds himself so vile that he does not desire to be his own law within himself, to enjoy things without himself, and to rise truly above himself, nay even to God Himself; or that he does not attempt to make use of all means offered, even the worst —thereby bringing himself to perdition and falling from the highest peak of dignity into the abyss of destruction. Thus there is nothing lacking in the facility of this matter for any man, but wise guidance.

Problem II

23. *To help man to recognize his own good and accustom himself to enjoy it.*

Let us imitate the school of Paradise, where God showed man the whole host of His creatures, that he might see that nothing else was like unto him, thus providing him with the opportunity of learning where the good adjudged him was not to be found, and of turning to the fountain-head. For there is no other way of enlightening man to the highest degree and leading him to know and enjoy the highest good, than to guide him from the circumference of things towards himself, as towards the centre in which all visible things are reflected; and from here to the ultimate goal of things, to God, towards whom all things visible and invisible tend. For if he is brought to see that only God excels all things, that He contains all things in Himself, and that He is the living fountain-head of all that is good, then (with God's help) he will be easily caught up, wrapt and absorbed, and will think himself blessed (being indeed so) to do and suffer only that which is His will.

Problem III

24. *It is easy to educate a reasonable creature to the use of reason.*

If anyone were to try to show a blind man the sun and the beauty of colour, or to teach a deaf man music, or a dumb beast to speak, etc., he would rightly be said to be acting foolishly, requiring activity from an agent to whom neither the possibility, nor the knowledge, nor the will needed for that activity has been given. But he is not acting foolishly who wants all men to be brought to that which they can and wish to be brought to, if only they are aware of it. Let them therefore learn to know it: then they will know it, wish it and be capable of it.

Problem IV

25. *To teach man to use things rightly.*

It is well enough known that true wisdom and our true blessedness lie in the true knowledge, understanding and use of things. If then all men learn to know things rightly and understand them aright, then they will easily learn to use them aright too. And this itself will bring about that the lost Paradise returns, i.e., that the whole world becomes a garden of delight for God, for us and for things. We know that this will come to be in eternity, but that it may be so at least imperfectly now, on the very threshold of eternity, at the end of the world, we must hope and long for, and with God's help bring about. Amen.

Problem V

26. *To make all men wise.*

Let all read the books of God, all understand them, and all practise and exercise them, and all will be wise, each according to the measure of the gift of Christ (Ephesians, IV. 7); for just as all vessels of every size thrown into the sea are filled with water, each according to its capacity, so the sea of God's wisdom (held in the banks of the world, the mind and the Scriptures) fills all the vessels of the souls dipped into it (see also Isaiah, LV. 10, 11).

Problem VI

27. *To banish all barbarism.*

No special art is required for this: if we but raise man from barbarism, i.e., from deadening conditions, and transfer him to where he has the opportunity to perceive different things with his senses, to consider different things with his reason, and to learn from report of different things lying beyond his view, then we soon see that brutes become men and that Anacharses are born in Scythia. What is to prevent us from extending this to all peoples? For he who is able to guide any one man across deserts and by labyrinthine ways, will be able to guide two, three, ten, a thousand or all men, if they come. If therefore we, or anybody else, are able to show one single man the true path of wisdom, virtue and salvation, then this one art, or be it prudence, will suffice to recall the whole world from darkness back to light, from error to truth, from destruction to salvation: for in these things, as long as they are the same, the measure is the same.

28. Let us end the demonstrations in this chapter with three conclusions:

(i) Nobody should be withheld, not to say driven away, from the pursuit of wisdom and the cultivation of the mind.

Unless we want to do injury not only to that one man, but to the whole of human nature, to the Father of this nature, God, who treats all in the same way, and finally to things themselves, which when the ignorant wrongly use them are destroyed along with them.

(ii) Nobody should hold himself apart and distant from education.

Unless he wants to do injury again not only to himself alone, but to human nature and to that society in which he must live (soundly, if wisely; disastrously, if foolishly); and to God (whose glory he cannot promote, if he stays as the beasts; but to whom he wreaks ignominy, from a man becoming a beast); and finally to things themselves which he has or will some day have beneath his dominion, for he will bring them to destruction.

(iii) Let all who are born men learn to live as men, or cease to be men.

But they cannot cease to be men, for they are the work of God's hand, and the works of the Lord are done in all truth; what has been done cannot be undone. Let such a man then return whence he wandered by his fall, that every man should indeed be that which he is called, a rational creature, with dominion over things, his own ruler and the delight of his Creator.

29. It is of course true that wisdom is required in the first place by those who are destined to teach, lead and rule others, by those who are to be philosophers, theologians, kings and magistrates. If however we weigh the matter on just scales, we see that precisely for this reason wisdom is needed by all men. For not only should every man be in the first place teacher, leader and ruler of himself, but he should be them for others too. For God gave every man commandment concerning his neighbour (Ecclesiasticus, XVII. 14), and that not only to love him (which is a general precept), but to teach the ignorant, recall him that errs, and admonish him that sins, etc.; Scripture is full of these commandments. Therefore there should be no man who is not a philosopher: for he was created a creature of reason and ordered to contemplate the nature of things and show them to others. There should be no man who is not a king: for he is destined to have dominion over the lesser creatures, over himself and those near to him. There should be no man who is not a priest: for it is his vocation to serve God his Creator both himself and on behalf of the lesser creatures, and his obligation to bring others to this service as well. There is therefore no man who does not need wisdom, although one man is placed in higher degree than another; no man can be utterly neglected.

30. It may be asked whether the blind, the deaf and the dull-witted, whose organic defect prevents them from being able to receive knowledge fully, should be admitted to education. I would answer: (1) Nothing is excluded from human education, unless it is no man. Therefore in so far as they partake of human nature, so far should they partake of education. Nay, all the more so, since they have greater need of external help, for nature on account of their internal defect can help them so much the less. (2) Especially since nature, when prevented from developing her full power in one direction, will develop it even more in some other direction, if only she is given help. For examples have clearly shown that men born blind have become famous musicians, lawyers, orators, etc., helped only by their hearing; while men born deaf have become excellent painters, sculptors, craftsmen, etc.; with the help of their feet men without hands have become fine scribes. And how much else! Since then access to the reasonable mind is always possible, light must be instilled by whatever path is provided. If indeed there is none— but I do not know whether there has ever been seen such a wooden

block that the soul creating an embryo, i.e., an habitation and organs, has not left herself any window to look out of or any way into herself— then he must be left in the hands of his Architect.

Chapter III

What is meant by saying that man should be educated
in all things that perfect human nature (1-12) ; why it is essential (13-30) ;
and how possible (31-32) and easy (33-48) it is.

1. Let that suffice to explain why it is necessary to educate all men. Now we must show:

(i) Not only some part of a man, but the whole man, must be educated in all things which go to perfect human nature.

(ii) This is possible in view of the nature of things.

(iii) Finally, how this may be achieved easily. Let us first set forth, however, whence so noble a wish was born and into what separate wishes it is resolved.

2. At the very beginning of the world intelligent men considered it an honour to come nearer to God by the glory of omniscience, being ignorant of nothing as far as this was possible. Not that such a desire sprang from morbid curiosity, but from the very creator of nature, God. He Himself at the very beginning, before the state of innocence was destroyed, gave our father Adam the chance to acquire some sort of systematic omniscience. Not only did He display before him a theatre of His wisdom with a wondrous variety of things, but gave His express command that he should observe these creatures, divide them into classes, and distinguish them one from another by giving them names. And are not all men the children of Adam ? And are we not heirs of his parental right ?

8

3. Later He also gave Solomon 'largeness of heart, even as the sand that is on the sea shore' (I Kings, iv. 29) so that he could expound all things in nature 'from the cedar tree even unto the hyssop'. The Book of Proverbs testifies that he could do the same in moral questions (assessing with perspicacity all human actions); so does the second book dealing with the fortuitous happenings of life, Ecclesiastes. Finally the Song of Solomon shows what love on the part of Christ for His church he observed in divine matters.

4. Many men have been seized with this desire for universal wisdom; the Greeks called such a system of omniscience ἐνκυκλοπαιδείαν (encyclopaedia), the Romans *doctrinarum orbem* (sphere of knowledge). Men of such encyclopaedic education have been known at various times. Among the Greeks the Sophists aped them, ready to discuss any subject at will without preparation; but the more severe philosophers, Socrates, Plato and others, combated this empty loquacity.

5. Nor is there today any lack of people who gather together all sound observations on all possible matters under the sun, and lay them before the public for their use, in systematic form, under the title of Encyclopaedias, Polymathias, Pandectas, Panaugias or even Pansophias, and similar universal titles. Nor is there any lack of great souls receiving with open arms what others offer with liberal hands, and rejoicing to fill their minds with universal knowledge universally acquired.

6. But we wish all men to receive encyclopaedic education, and not only some; and not only to be instructed in all things which it is possible to know, but in all that they need to do and to explain in speech; so that by those gifts which distinguish man from the beasts, reason, speech and divers free manipulation of things, man should be as far removed from them as possible. For reason is that divine light in man by which, seeing within himself and other things without himself, he can contemplate, and contemplating can judge. Hence is born directly love of that which is good, or will, by which man follows whatever good he senses in things, extending his longing ever forward into the future, nay even into eternity. Speech is the flowing out of this light from one man to another, by which he passes on and explains clearly and distinctly for the understanding of others that which he himself has understood. Finally action is the faculty of carrying out those things he has understood and spoken, if he wishes, with wonderful skill.

7. Well did the Christian philosopher write: 'God has equipped man with three tools: mind with which to invent what is necessary; words as

a helper; hands with which to carry out all that he has either thought out with his mind or learned from the words of others' (Cardanus, Lib. de subt. xi). Nor could it be otherwise than that the creature destined to have dominion over the other creatures should be provided with mind for the wise observation of all things, with tongue for communication to others of all that his mind acknowledges and decides, and with hands and other efficient members to carry out his decisions.

8. That man was so created, and that at his creation he was straightway called to these three functions, is testified by holy history. It is written that man, who was created to have dominion over all creatures (Genesis, I. 28), had brought unto him all the creatures of the earth that he might see them (Genesis, II. 19) and straightway call them by their names (ibid.), and finally that he was placed in the Garden of Eden to dress it and keep it (v. 15). Behold here the three functions: to see, to name and to do.

9. For up to now all that man does can be and is reduced to these three: thoughts, words, deeds; and God has warned all men that they will be questioned as to these three things on the last day. Thus he said wisely who said: 'The salt of wisdom must be sought in school, i.e. to know, to do, to speak.' This is what we should like to extend to all men, that in this way Christ's words might be fulfilled: 'Every one shall be salted with salt' (Mark, IX. 49).

10. And since every man, in so far as he is a man, is called upon to have three kinds of converse in this world (as we have seen in Pansophy), it is necessary to consider how he may be made capable of these three kinds of converse, and how to ensure it. First man has converse with the lower creatures, that he may know and use them. Then he has converse with men, who partake of the same nature, that he may live in peace with them for mutual benefit. Finally he has converse with the ruler of all things, God himself, that by His grace he may attain the love, guidance and protection of God, and finally be blessed to all eternity. Thus the prerogative of human nature can be resolved into five parts:

(i)   To rule by the mind and wisdom;
(ii) To bear weight by the tongue and eloquence;
(iii) To be capable of action;
(iv) To be of good morals and behaviour;
(v) Finally by the grace of God to be devout in this world and in eternity to be worthy by His grace of abiding with Him in blessedness.

11. Finally then, if we consider the innate desires of man altogether, education for humanity falls into twelve parts; for everyone born man, by reason of the most intimate impulses of his nature, longs:

(i)   To be, i.e., to live;

(ii) To live unshakeably, i.e., to be of worth;

(iii) To live observantly, i.e., to know what he has around him;

(iv) To live by light, i.e., to understand what he knows;

(v)   To live in freedom, i.e., to desire and choose what he knows to be good, not to wish but to refuse what is bad, and to act in all things according to his own judgement, if possible;

(vi) To live actively, i.e., to perform that which he understands and chooses, so as not to understand and choose in vain;

(vii) To have or to possess much;

(viii) To enjoy all he has in security;

(ix) To be eminent and held in honour;

(x)   To be as eloquent as possible in order to convey his knowledge and his will to others promptly and clearly;

(xi) To enjoy the favour and grace of men, so that they do not envy him, but wish him as quiet, happy and untroubled life as possible;

(xii) Finally to enjoy the favour of God, for joy of heart and for the assurance of his happiness in God.

12. Behold, it is clear what are 'all things' in which human nature is to be educated! They are not things snatched in bold usurpation, but granted to us by the divine will itself. For they are so deeply imprinted in human nature that there is no man who (even if he wished) could deprive himself of any one of them, as long as he remains in his right mind. If a man seem to neglect these desires of his soul, and let them sleep; make him feel that danger threatens his life, his health, his liberty, his possessions or his honour; or that he is unable to perceive, understand or carry out something concerning himself; or that the use of his goods is taken from him; or that instead of the favour of man and God he is the object of the hatred and envy of men and the wrath and wounds of the Lord: how quickly will you see him bestir himself! So much does the whole perfection of man consist in these things altogether.

13. I declare therefore that all men should be brought to all these things by diligent education, since (1) it is altogether in the interests of (a) God, (b) man and (c) things themselves; (2) it is within the power of everyone born human; (3) it is also easy if the matter is approached with

reason, granted the favour of God. Let us put forward these points separately one after the other.

14. Man is called the glory of God, because he is the image of God (I Corinthians, XI. 7). And the more like a picture is to its model, the more glorious it is; if it bear no resemblance to that model it is no image but a monstrosity, to the shame and not to the glory of its maker. Wherefore the Scriptures write: 'For all have sinned, and come short of the glory of God' (Romans, III. 23). Therefore that they may not come short of the glory of God and thus rob God of his glory, all must be taught not to sin, not to err and not to fail in any thing in which they should be like God. The most eminent virtues of God being (1) Omniscience, (2) Omnipotence, (3) Utter Holiness, (4) All-sufficiency, then it is certain that the man in whom wisdom, virtue and holiness are visibly resplendent, and who suffices unto himself (after God), is the true image of God and the true glory of his Creator. Oh, let all the earth then be filled with the glory of the Lord (Numbers, XIV. 21), the tabernacle of the Church (Exodus, XL. 34) and all the hearts of the faithful be filled with all the fulness of God (Ephesians, III. 19).

15. As for man, since such profound longings are born in his heart to attain his full perfection (as we have seen in paragraph 11), we may not wish them to be frustrated in any man, unless we wish wilfully to destroy the work of God in us and envy any man his happiness. Far be it from us! Rather ought we to help every man to his highest good (in the service of God's bounty). I will say something of each point.

16. Man must be taught so to love this present life as to wish it eternal. I do not say that they should be taught to love life and living, for this possession is so common to all living things that it is not necessary to teach men to love life; it is rather necessary to dissuade, for out of too great love for life many men sin their whole life. But they should love this present life in such a way that if anything else comes after it will be life and not death. Otherwise, if life is to pass into death, it were better not to be born.

17. It is in the interests of every man to take proper care for his health. For if the house of clay of the human body, in which the heavenly guest stays, be faulty, incomplete, or weak, in any of its parts, what can the guest do but languish himself and suffer his functions to be impeded? Rightly then the poet said: 'Let us beg for a healthy mind in a healthy body'. For the foundation of action is an active life, i.e., vigorous health. Therefore it is necessary to pay attention to health all through life, but

especially at the beginning of life, lest the seeds of disease planted in youth bring an ill harvest in old age; for evil neglected at the start becomes incurable.

18. It is of great importance to bring men to the knowledge of many things, so that they understand whatever can be perceived by the senses, reason and faith; thus gaps in the mind and hence in the will and in our deeds can be prevented, such as spring from ignorance of necessary things. For all things exist for man, and for his use; but they can be of no use to him unless he uses them for something; and he cannot use them unless he knows them. In this matter the words of Sirachovec are apposite: 'In great as in small things be not ignorant in anything' (Ch. 5. 18).

19. But it is not enough to have an external knowledge of things; man must be brought to the inner understanding of things in order to avoid those errors which spring from superficial observation without closer knowledge of things. The world is full of such errors, for the common run of men merely touch upon the surface of the things they meet, using their senses alone, and not penetrating into the vitals. And since they do not understand things, but want to look as though they understand, monstrous ideas are born, and manifold chaos in opinions and errors, which drives the world to dizzy fall. There is no other remedy for this but knowledge of the innermost constitution of things; this was the aim of Pansophy, while Pampaedia (universal education) seeks to instil this knowledge into the soul.

20. It is important that man should learn and be able to choose and dispose freely of things rightly understood, according to his own judgement, that the divine image in man should never be destroyed, least of all in that matter in which it reaches its highest point, in freedom of choice. If this is taken away, and man forced to submit his will to the decision of others, then will becomes nil and man is man no longer. In this sense Seneca said: 'Men perish by example, for they would rather believe than judge (and thus are led by the will of others rather than by their own), and follow the flock of those who have gone before, in the manner of beasts, going not the way they should go but the way others go.' Since this great calamity, like the universal flood, overtaking all the truth and goodness of things together with human judgement and freedom, has made the world grow dull, a universal remedy is required. And no other can be found but that man, giving up this habit of following others like the beasts, should learn to place before his will, like the

clearest torch, none other than God, things, and his senses rightly formed and guided by things, and then to be led by this light. For only this will mean following none other but God and his guidance (I mean the guidance of God's word, His hands and His impulse) and appearing as the true image of God. Those who respect human authority too highly forget that they too are men, and surrender their own judgement, the primary gift of human nature. Those on the other hand who force others to accept their views, demanding blind assent and obedience, violate human nature. Cicero declared that 'the search for truth is proper to man'. If it is proper to man, then it may not be separated from human nature. It must be admitted that it has been said for all who are men: 'Prove all things and hold to that which is good'.

21. It is also very important for humanity that men should become zealous and industrious, for not only in Sodom was idleness the first occasion for corruption (Ezekiel, XVI. 49); the depravities of the whole world spring from this first cause, so much so that even the first sin in the Garden of Eden was born of Eve's idle wandering. Wherefore the first antidote to sin prescribed for man before the fall was to observe living creatures and to cultivate the garden (Genesis, II. 15, 19), and after the fall as a remedy for an even greater ill sweat was given to him, that is to say hard work (Genesis, III. 19); both remedies indeed, shown to man by a doctor indeed. Human wisdom has recognized this among the heathen too, and many sayings bear witness in this matter, such as these: 'Idleness is the root of all evil'; 'Idleness and inaction destroy man's life and strength'; 'Idleness breeds disease'; 'Idleness is evil through and through'; 'You ask why Aegisthos was an adulterer? The answer's clear: he was an idler!' And many more. Examples from whole nations teach us that wherever honest labour flourishes, there vice does not share the throne. For if each man goes silently about his work and all have enough through their zeal, then none are poor, none have time for wickedness. The contrary can indeed be seen where men give themselves up to laziness and idle ease. Therefore from this point of view, too, the world would be blessed if men were all schooled in earnest industry.

22. It would be well for men to have great possessions (each according to his needs) and for all to learn the art of being rich. That is to say, all men should know how to have a sufficiency, not to be in want and therefore not to covet the goods of others, nor to disturb the peace by this covetousness. Oh, how peaceful would it be in the world if all were to live content with themselves and their possessions, and nobody to

bring lawsuits about mine and thine ! Every man under his vine and under his fig tree, as in the days of Solomon (I Kings, IV. 25).

23. It would be well for all men to be able to live in safety, wherefore all should be taught how to achieve this. By safety I mean the tranquillity of an honest mind, arising from the calm and peaceful use and enjoyment of possessions. Not all are granted this enjoyment in the tumultuous state of worldly affairs, even if one and the other hedge themselves about with privileges against the unlawful attacks of kings.

24. It would be well for all men to live in honour and none to suffer ignominy; for one thing, man is the most eminent of all creatures and most honoured by God; for another, impatient of ignominy he is easily moved to avenge contempt. Hence swarm quarrels, wars, murders and endless other troubles; it would be well to prevent them, no man's dignity as a man suffering thereby.

25. It would be well for no man to be dumb, but for all to be able to explain their needs to God and to men. For man was not made to be a dumb statue, but was given a tongue with which to sing the praises of his Creator and to bring his neighbours to partake of the light with him, by giving them the right information about whatever is needful.

26. All men should be educated to be of quiet manners, so that those who are naturally of good character should not be corrupted, while those who are evil should be recalled to righteousness. For the poet truly said:

'There is none so wild but cannot be tamed
If he will but lend a patient ear.'

27. The most important thing for all men, however, is for the soul to be imbued with piety before all, among all and after all, to win God's favour, without whose will man is nought. If we do not succeed in this whatever else we endeavour we shall be but as squirrels imprisoned in the cage of our own vanity, and the more busily we concern ourselves with external skills and the things of this life, the more we shall tire and yet we shall never manage to get out of the cage of the world. But the devout exercise of piety will give us wings on which to rise swiftly above the machine of this world, whenever we please, and enjoy eternal delight with God. Hence it was not in vain that Moses noted down that the godless children of Cain spent their time inventing external skills (and particularly the first bastards in the world, the sons of Lamech begotten in bigamy); while the pious sons of Seth began to call upon the name of

the Lord (Genesis, IV. 17 to end); dominion over other men was first started by Nimrod, the grandson of Ham (Genesis, x. 8). Wherefore Christ, setting out to reform the world and to turn us from vain, or at least too worldly occupations to eternal cares, did not instruct Himself nor His apostles in the sciences; but He filled them with the spirit of wisdom and fear of the Lord, that it might be clear that only through piety lies man's way to his final goal, and that this is the one necessary thing without which all the rest is nothing and achieves nothing. This is that of which He spoke when He said to Martha, troubled about many things, 'One thing is needful' (Luke, x. 42). Therefore all the other things mortals strive for, if this one be taken away, are but childish games. For just as games of all kinds are for the idle or for those who seek only recreation, and contribute nothing to the work in hand; and just as he who does not know how to play, knowing only what is needful for life, is not abused; so the external arts and sciences provide the mind only with pleasant excursions, but not with satisfaction, for they do not meet man's deepest longings. For if a man should know nothing of science, but should know Christ; or if he should be wise for heaven and not for the world; then is he all the wiser. Therefore must we before all, among all and after all recommend to all men to strive for the wisdom of Heaven, piety.

28. Thus far we have devoted ourselves to explaining why it is in the interests of God and of man that all men should be educated in all things; now let us add that it is in the interest of those things themselves which are subject to human rule, to be administered only by wise men (and that by utterly wise men). For any man may come across any thing whatsoever, but unless he is able to handle that thing according to the nature of it, he will not be able to do anything with it. And then the nature of things will suffer violence and groan beneath the yoke, and lament that it is subjected to vanity, being willing to serve, but unable to serve when dealt with ignorantly. (Compare this with what was said in the previous chapter, paragraph 13.)

29. If any man say: Let the craftsman carry on his craft, and each man work in his own sphere; why is it necessary to teach all men all things ? I would answer: Nature, the mother of things, forms the same members for every man to be (in his mother's womb): feet, hands, eyes, tongue: although not all men will become runners, scribes, observers, orators, etc. But since all these things are human activities she forms a complete man, taking care of all human needs once and for all. Why should we not

do the same as far as possible, when forming him for the second time (which is our skill), so that no man should carry about with him useless tools he does not know how to use? For barbarians carry about with them uselessly all their tools: the senses, talent, judgement, memory, tongue and heart; and so does any uneducated man, carrying along with him any untrained faculty.

30. If anyone goes on: Are we therefore to bring all men to the knowledge of evil too, that they may be experienced in all things? I would answer: (1) The theoretical knowledge of evil is not in itself evil, as can be seen from the example of God and the holy angels, who are acquainted with evil but are not therefore evil themselves. (2) For us too this knowledge is good and useful, that by true knowledge of evil we should be deterred from real evil. Therefore God straightaway showed the first man the tree of the knowledge of good and evil; that he should not know them? Nay, but that he should know and beware. (3) But since we are already corrupt and things observed move the senses, it is certainly safer not to know evil. How to avoid teaching people evil will be set out later, in paragraph 48.

31. So far we have discussed why it is desirable for all men to have the chance of full education; now we must inquire whether it is also possible. Why should it not be? Since every man is so formed as to show God, being His image. This is shown by the faculties placed in the human soul by nature herself: the desire always (1) to know different things; (2) to build them; (3) to appear pious, just and good in everything we do; (4) and finally to depend as little as possible on others and entirely on ourselves, if that is possible. For where is the man who would not hold it his glory to know much, to be able to do much, to be good (or certainly to seem to be) and to be self-sufficient (not needing others)? Whence come these impulses? Or did He who gave us such will not wish to add the possibility too, or could He not?

32. For to these inborn desires have there not been added also the means by which man, if he use them, may attain those desires? Since it is not of the wisdom of God to set ends without providing the means, it is clear that for the twelve desires of our hearts (set out in paragraph 11) as many possibilities of attaining them have been provided, if only they are observed; or of losing them, if these possibilities are ignored.

For (i) the life of the body is a matter of organs, capable of being preserved or injured according as the organs are preserved or injured.

(ii) The health of the body consists in the firm coherence of its parts and the preservation of each of them in full vigour; it can therefore be preserved, if corrupting influences are avoided.

(iii) It is possible to know all things which are set out in the three books of God and for the purpose of finding which we were given the organs of sense, reason and faith. For through our external senses the whole of the external world enters into us; through reason we can investigate those things of which the greater part lies hidden; and through faith we can comprehend whatever is hidden but which it pleases God to reveal. What do we lack to be able to gain the treasure of some sort of omniscience?

(iv) It is also possible to understand everything that has causes for its being, and these have all things; if they are not clearly set out, they are certainly to be grasped from indications. Work is all that is required; in most cases there is no impossibility.

(v) To whom is it not given to judge and choose the things which he has understood? Surely all do it, not only those who have truly understood, but those who think they have understood too; and indeed even among fools who does not burn with desire to use things as he thinks fit without having understood them?

(vi) Man can carry out everything for which he has been provided with organs; but for what has he not been provided?

(vii) Why should it not be possible to have whatever good things there may be? God has so richly furnished the house He has lent us for our habitation, the world, that there is abundance of everything needful for all of us, if only we know enough.

(viii) Every man can enjoy all things which attract him by whatever good he sees in them; but which of the works of God cannot thus attract him? For all things are good, each in its own time (Sirachovec 39. 26, 40).

(ix) Every man can achieve eminence, if only he knows the real meaning of eminence, and the right road to reach the heights. For by the very right of creation we have dominion over all visible creatures (Psalm 8. 6, 7), by the blessing of redemption we excel even above the angels (Hebrews, 11. 16) and finally through sanctification we are raised to be partakers of the divine nature (II Peter, 1. 4). Are these not great things?

(x) Any man who has been given by God a sound mind, a tongue and ears, can become eloquent; and surely only few have been deprived of these organs by unhappy chance.

(xi) Every man who has learned the laws of decorum and the gift of peace, both within his own soul and towards his neighbours, can adorn himself with good behaviour and the favour of men; and who could fail to learn them?

(xii) Finally to be joined with God in love and obedience is possible for every man who has tasted the sweetness of the highest good, which exists in God alone as its source and emanates from Him to all men and all things. But why should we not try to make it possible for all men to taste it? For the voice of God says: 'O taste and see that the Lord is good' (Psalm 34. 8).

Nothing remains to be done, then, but to see how the possibility of such desirable things could be made facility; we will now consider this in the form of problems.

General Problem

34. *To help men to achieve all their desires.*

(1) The sense of natural desire must be aroused in them. (2) They must be shown the way to achieve fulfilment in order to arouse the hope of possibility. (3) Finally by examples taken from themselves and others they must be shown how easily this may be done. All these things will now be dealt with one by one.

Special Problem I

35. *To bring man to love and care for the future life.*

We must diligently show that after this life there is something else, either life eternal if we succeed in joining the fountain of life, which is God; or death eternal, if we stray from the fountain of life. For just as we have all passed through our first abode in our mother's womb (where we were prepared for the customs of this present life); and just as we are all passing through our second home beneath the heavens (in order to be prepared for the future life); so surely shall we all come to our third abode, which is eternity itself, whence there is no going out, whether we see ourselves raised to eternal light or flung into eternal darkness.

124

But no man wishes to be thrown into darkness; all long to be admitted to the fount of joy and light. Let all therefore admit that

(i) Nothing is so necessary to man as to know what he needs for life both here and hereafter;

(ii) The wisest man is he that is wise for eternity. God testifies that wisdom is provision for the future (Deuteronomy, XXXII. 29). And the most future and last of all things is eternity.

(iii) That man is doubly wise who even in this world is not lacking in wisdom (for it is better to participate in good always and everywhere than only sometimes and somewhere).

Problem II

36. *To pass through this life in such a way, as to arrive in eternity.*

This will be achieved if men learn to make use of this life, and not only enjoy it; in this way our present transitory life will be not only the precursor but also the preparation for the future eternal life. This will be so if men grow accustomed to know, choose and do in this life mainly those things the knowledge, sweetness and treasure of which cannot be fulfilled but in blessed eternity. All men will know what these things are, if all are taught; all men will choose them, if they perceive aright that in these lies their highest good and are not blinded by transient values; and all men will do everything to gain such a high goal, if all rightly recognize the road to eternal felicity, which is hard and narrow, but pleasant. Though we may scarce hope for all this (such is human blindness and malice), yet if we but try we shall be doing that which is to the glory of God and the good of man.

Conclusion:

It will be best for man to show him the differences between the two lives, in as varied and accurate a way as possible. The present life is one of motion, the future one of calm; the former is therefore transitory, the latter permanent; the former short, the latter everlasting without end; the former stormy and troubled, the latter calm and peaceful; the former ambiguous and dangerous, the latter firm and safe; and finally the former is but the journey towards the latter life, encumbered by impediments, diversions and delays. Or to show that those who hasten to their heaven-

ly homeland must sail across the sea beset with rocks and shallows and
storms. Therefore we must see to it with the utmost care and anxiety
that not one of those travelling to his heavenly home meet the fate so
often suffered by those sailing to an earthly land: for the waves of the
sea carry them elsewhere than they intend, nay, even into the hands of
their enemies; or the fury of the storm swallows them in shipwreck.

Problem III

37. *To enjoy constant good health in this life.*
The way to achieve this is easy if you flee that which injures health,
use that which preserves health, and are not overdelicate but hard-
working, pious and devoted to God. If it should befall you otherwise,
honour your doctor for the sake of the Lord Who made him (Sirachovec,
38. 1).
The dangers to health from outside are all dangerous falls, blows and
wounds; from inside all excesses, whether of heat or cold, movement or
calm (i.e., torpor and lassitude), over-eating or over-drinking, or again
excessive emptiness whether on account of hunger, fasting or medicines, etc.
Health is preserved by a well-ordered life in respect to food, exercise,
sleep and all those things mentioned above, where only excess or dearth
are harmful, while moderate use is beneficial. Give your stomach the
proper food in the proper way. Give your body its due degree of movement and quiet; give your mind due recreation and honest solace; give
God the honour which is His due, setting Him up firmly as the Lord of
your life, and worshipping him always. Be devout, not to rouse his anger;
lest men be roused against you, deal with all men kindly; and then you
may well hope. Particularly if you get accustomed to opposites (according
to Cornelius Celsus, the first doctor among the Romans): tolerating
both heat and cold, both labour and rest, eating a little more and then
fasting again, sleeping a long time and then keeping awake a long time,
alternately. In this way it is easy to avoid illness, i.e., disturbance of
function, if nature becomes accustomed to all things whatsoever. But,
as Celsus adds, we should take care to lean more often to the more
beneficial side, i.e., eating more often than fasting, sleeping more and
keeping awake less doggedly.

Problem IV

38. *To make anyone understand everything.*

(1) Present sensual objects to the senses, each to its proper sense for direct experience (autopsia); and (2) reduce mental concepts to sensual concepts through parables or symbols; and (3) demonstrate evidence of testimony by direct demonstration ('αυτοπιζίαν) and straightway it will come about that the senses will perceive their object, reason will understand it, and faith will acquiesce with its light—for the senses are the door through which the external world enters into us, with all which it contains; reason is the door through which man enters himself as the image of God, to see within himself numbers, measures, and weights, with the help of which he penetrates the heart of things, even remote and abstruse things; faith is the door through which the word of God enters, and God Himself, with His eternity. Behold, thus is man made, that he can hold all things if he is offered them. The eye is not sated with vision nor the ear with hearing, nor the other senses with their objects, nor the memory with all the senses bring it, if they only bring experience and do not stuff it in. Here we may place Aristotle's clean tablet, to which he compared the capacity of the human mind; for although there is nothing inscribed on our minds when we come into the world, all things can be written there (by the action of the senses, reason and faith). But the comparison is a halting one, for a tablet is a corporeal thing, finite, which can be filled until there is no room for more. But the mind of man, bearing the mark of his Creator (infinitude), cannot be so filled with a multitude of objects that it is not capable of containing still more. For such a great gift we owe God endless praise.

Problem V

39. *To succeed in making all things understood.*

The understanding of things arises from the right comprehension of the causes of things. Therefore if you want a man to understand something you must explain clearly (that he may see it with his eyes) (1) what the thing is (by means of the nearest kind and the nearest mark of differentiation, usually taken from the nearest end); (2) whence it comes (by material and effectual cause); (3) in what manner it exists (by the inner form and the bonds which bind all in one whole). If these things are rightly understood, the thing will be understood.

Problem VI

40. *For men to use their free will rightly.*

Human nature is so formed that in all things man wishes to act according to his own will, not to be forced—nor can he be, without violation of his nature. Among the arguments for this point is the desire of every man to learn what has been, is and will be, whence springs the love of history, the turning of the senses outward to all things around, admiration for the prophets and zeal for the study of divinity. The foundation of this is the fact that man, made lord over things, longs to direct all things, even the events of the future, by his present perspicacity. And if he cannot direct them beforehand, at least to know them in advance; and if not even that, then at least he wants to know how they came about; and that not simply, like a spectator who is not concerned, but as an arbiter and judge of things subjected to his rule. For man takes unto himself the right to approve what is well done and blame what is ill done in all things he sees developing before his eyes or already completed; thus he plays the censor, nor can he do otherwise. Behold the indelible sign of the superiority of human nature, power in all things! And the basis for the freest action in all things. Therefore:

(i) Let all be allowed to judge things, but things they have truly understood.

(ii) Let them be allowed to use free choice, but after they have first clearly understood the distinction between good and evil (better and worse, best and worst), that it be clear we do not err through our minds.

(iii) Let them be allowed to follow their own choice, but where it is clear that they have chosen the better, not the worse.

If such human liberty flourished everywhere that all things were filled with order and light, and if the torrent of coercion and violence were replaced by the stream of spontaneous acts, then peace and security would ensue.

J. A. COMENII
JANUA LINGUARUM
RESERATA QUINQUE-LINGUIS.

Sive compendiosa Methodus

LATINAM, GALLICAM, ITALICAM,
HISPANICAM & GERMANICAM
Linguam perdiscendi,

Sub Titulis centum , Periodis mille comprehensa ; &
Vocabulis bis mille ad minimum aucta.

Cum quintuplici Indice,

A NATHANAELE DUESIO.

In Idioma Gallicum & Italicum translata, & in hac Tertia
Editione accuratè emendata atque correcta.

Cum interpretatione Hispanica G. R.

AMSTELODAMI,
Apud Ludovicum & Danielem Elzevirios.
cIɔ Iɔc LXI.

Cum gratia & privilegio Sacra Casarea Majestatis.

Title page of *Janua Linguarum* (Amsterdam edition).

Problem VII

41. Human nature is lively, rejoicing in movement and action, and needing nothing but prudent guidance. Just as the mind is always thinking about something, and the will is always making some choice, so the executive faculties cannot but busy themselves with carrying out those thoughts and decisions. There is no need of outward stimulus, for we carry them within ourselves; only guidance is needed, lest inordinate impulse should go too far. These three recommendations are meant to further this:

(i) To begin early to train movement and action; this in order to acquire agility, which is not easily lost if consolidated by practice. Therefore boys should be allowed to play games and run, always doing something, as long as it is never immodest.

(ii) To learn to do everything they undertake seriously, i.e., earnestly and not hesitatingly.

(iii) To do everything for some end, whether serious or playful, for the sake of praise or victory. It will be the foundation of a good mind not to be concerned with vanities but to train for difficult tasks, placing some goal ahead. For our soul is like a flame, the more vehement it is, the more effective. Let men therefore accustom themselves to do all things with some goal in sight, holding it beneath their dignity to be carried along at random and busy with trifles. Unless from time to time through lack of more urgent tasks they prefer to busy themselves with less important things, rather than to do nothing in laziness. For there it is a grave matter, to avoid idleness, the snare of Satan.

Problem VIII

42. *To accomplish that men should not live in need, but rather in abundance.*

The ever-good God always distributes His largesse, if only we lack not hands to receive. Nor is our nature insatiable in itself, the opinion of only some people at some times. Nay, it is more blessed to live on little, for life is less distracted thereby. Otherwise, whom God and his own virtue does not suffice, nothing will suffice.

9

The art of growing rich, however, consists in three things: to pray, to work and to be grateful. Why should not men learn these three things?

(i) In the first place we must pray to God, that when He gives to all he should not deny us; for we have the divine promise 'He who asks, to him shall be given.'

(ii) Secondly, since this promise was given to them that seek and knock, we must not wait for the gifts of God to fall from heaven into idle hands; we must plough the earth, cultivate the garden, pasture flocks, etc., i.e., each must work diligently in his own station. Then the words of Truth will indeed be true: He that seeketh findeth and to him that knocketh it shall be opened.

(iii) Finally, whatever is given to him that seeks and knocks, we must accept with grateful hand; lest God be offended by our ingratitude and withdraw His blessing, or even retract that which He has already given. For not in vain has it been said: 'Unto every one which hath shall be given; and from him that hath not, even that he hath shall be taken away from him.' (Luke, XIX. 26).

In short: (i) Seek the source rather than the stream, God rather than riches. (ii) By your labour prepare a passage from this source into your garden. (iii) Whatever flows along it accept, and use in gratitude.

Problem IX

43. *Render men happy in their possessions and secure from misfortune.*

The first can be achieved if men learn to use and not to abuse their possessions; the second by taking care not to anger, and by angering rouse against yourself, either God, your own self or any man. And since God is angered by sin, our souls by evil desires, and a mind conscious of evil, and men by insolent attacks, whoever takes extreme care to avoid these three things, can enjoy his possessions in pleasant security. But if anything should turn out otherwise, then it must be patiently borne, bearing in mind the lot of man beneath the heavens and the great wisdom of divine providence, ordaining all things for the best for His people in the end.

Problem X

44. *To live in honour.*

There are three infallible means to gain this end. (1) If a man allows no dishonourable thing towards himself, any other man, or any thing. (2) If he seek not to seem but to be. (3) If he look in these things not to men, but to God, the upholder of truth, and his own conscience, his most intimate witness—according to the well-known lines:

'Each man is a world unto himself; then seek not thyself elsewhere.'

If you are indeed such a man, you will be held in honour by God as His most proper image, as well as by the angels and by all good men, whether you live in the public eye or in seclusion. For here it is not to the point whether the common throng and multitude hold you in honour or not; for the crowd does not understand the matter, often adoring the cloaca for the altar. Take no account of them and seek true honour, which is to be found enthroned in virtue alone.

Problem XI

46. *Render every man eloquent.*

If you are not thinking of loquacity (which is due more to nature than to training) but of the ability to express thoughts suitably in speech, then this can be promised to any man who has learned to distinguish one thing from another correctly with his mind and give the right name to each of them, and to connect words together aptly. For then you are able to talk sense and not nonsense, to use words and not monstrosities of words, to put together a coherent speech, not sand without lime. Thus in the end even the simplest of men, little gifted for speaking, can become eloquent; to God in perpetual sighs, to man in truly simple and truthful words: Yes, yes, no, no, etc.

Problem XII

46. (sic) *To educate men to be of good behaviour and kindness.*

The foundation of good behaviour is either self-control or the toleration of control by others. The first implies that man should be accustomed to do nothing on impulse, but all with reason; in the words of Claudian:

'Not until then will you rightly possess all things—
When you can be your own king ...'

But since man while young does not yet possess such clear reasoning powers as to be able to distinguish everywhere around him what is profitable, through lack of experience, the second foundation of good behaviour and honourable life has been added, the toleration of the rule of others. For just as nothing can act rightly which is not itself right, so men should first grow accustomed to being ruled, and then to rule; and that first themselves, and then other men and other things. Both can be readily achieved by the same method: (1) enlightenment must be given in constant examples, both from history and from the present day; (2) the reasons for following one thing and fleeing another must be explained by accurate precepts. They must be urged to put these principles into practice continuously and with care; not by harsh and violent words, but by calm and willing guidance. In this way all men can be persuaded to use civility.

Problem XIII

47. *To instil piety in man's soul effectively.*

It is clear from the Scriptures that piety itself is a thing to be acquired through discipline, i.e., not immediately or miraculously sent from God, but acquired by the regular way of education. Otherwise God would not have praised Abraham for commanding his household to piety (Genesis, XVIII. 19); nor would He have laid it upon parents so often to bring up their children in discipline and in the admonition of the Lord (Deuteronomy, VI. 20, Ephesians, VI. 4. et al.). And why should piety not be acquired through training? For (i) examples are not lacking; in the first place that of God Himself, who said 'Be ye holy, even as I am holy', and of His Son Jesus Christ, who was made man that He might teach men by everlasting examples how they ought to behave on all occasions. Secondary examples of piety are provided by the angels (of whom so much has been told so that we might learn to imitate the way they serve God), and all holy men of both Testaments, like little stars in the spiritual heaven of the Church, shining with beauteous light (after the sun of justice itself).

(ii) Nor is there any lack of precepts and rules for the training of piety; they are scattered throughout the Holy Scriptures, whence wise and pious men have collected them and must still collect them.

(iii) Nor, finally, is there any lack of ways by which we should practise this piety daily and correct any lapses we discover, until the perfect man of God is formed, 'thoroughly furnished unto all good works' (II Timothy, III. 17). Therefore we must (1) start young, before the tender soul has met with real corruption. For God has testified that only this tender age is suitable for this intimate training (Isaiah, XXVIII. 9). And Christ said 'of such is the kingdom of God' (Mark, X. 14); (2) constant examples must be presented first, from their own and others' experience; on every given occasion and in every possible case the example of Christ and the saints should be quoted; (3) constantly urge imitation, adding from time to time precepts and rules, and divine promises and comminations. Finally prayers for them and with them must be poured out to God. If all these are earnest, then the promise of Christ (Mark, IV. 24) can be earnestly hoped for.

Problem XIV

48. *No man should learn evil things, from himself, or others, and still less from his teachers.*

Every idler, left to the images of his imagination, will learn evil from himself; from others, if he mixes with bad company or is given the chance of seeing, hearing or doing evil; and finally from his preceptor and master, whoever is taught strange skills or learned in pagan books. Therefore

(i) All men should be occupied with good things, that they may not have leisure to sin. Whence come the words: He who would avoid vice must avoid idleness.

(ii) Society should not be allowed unless it be good. Therefore the fellowship of evil men should be fled, and if possible abolished. If we cannot do this, and it some time inevitably happen that we come across such things, we should avert our eyes, shut our ears and hasten away. And if we should catch sight of something, seeing and even touching pitch, we must wash our hands, clear our conscience and make firmer resolve ever to flee such things.

(iii) Men should be taught to learn all things which can be to their good, and not to learn whatever it is harmful to know. Therefore they should be given the opportunity to learn the former and denied the opportunity to learn the latter. For whatever you present to the senses will be understood; what you do not present will not be understood; just as a mirror reflects whatever is placed before it (the sky or the earth) and nothing else. Therefore evil books and scandalous pictures must be destroyed, and all occasions for evil.

(iv) If it is impossible not to know something, and the simple knowledge would be harmful, then the knowledge should only be allowed together with the antidote. (For example, in reading the Bible, Cain's murder, Lamech's bigamy, Lot's incest, must be read with the punishment that followed them.)

49. Let the Apostle bring our desires to a close: that we should pray and strive that our 'whole spirit and soul and body be preserved blameless unto the coming of our Lord Jesus Christ' (I Thessalonians, v. 23). For this would mean educating the whole man, not a part of him, if we see to it that no man lacks those things which sustain the body, feed the mind (the arts and sciences) and finally preserve for eternal life the soul (our highest part, through which we are the image of God).

Chapter IV

What is meant by educating all men in all ways to all things (1);
what purpose it serves (2-6); and how possible (7-11) and easy (12-18) it is.
Transition to the following chapters (19-22).

I have already said that we must show how to make a start on the education of the human race so that not only all men may be educated to all things, but that in all ways they may be educated and cultured. But what do we mean by education in all ways? Not education for appearance's sake, but in truth, to the real profit of this life and the next. So that every man trained to wisdom, eloquence, science, manners, civility and piety should become not curious, but informed; not talkative, but eloquent; not a boastful beginner of tasks, but an efficient man at carrying them out; not a mask of virtue, but virtue itself; and finally not a hypocrite affecting piety, but a pious and holy worshipper of God in the spirit and the truth.

2. If our proposals for universal education do not tend towards this end we are wasting our time, deceiving God and ourselves and contributing nothing to the reform of affairs both private and public; it would be better to relinquish the whole plan than to attempt it to no purpose. For what has the world gained by the superficial knowledge of things? It has only become crazed with the charm of opinions and wholly infected with the poison of various errors. What has it gained by garrulous loquacity, however witty? It has only become full of endless trivialities for vain amusement, and completely tied up in endless litigious quarrels for mutual hatred. What has it gained by so many works and inventions ingenious for vanity but most of them useless for the true glory of God and the salvation of man? It has only become a theatre of vanity, feeding on the empty smoke of vanity. What has it gained by polished elegance of manners and Machiavellian skill in controlling men? It has only become a place where all wear masks and no man trusts his neighbour, for everything is full of cunning, fraud and deceit, and therefore full of simulation and dissimulation, guile and trickery; nor can any trust be placed in promises, pacts, pledges, seals, agreements, testimony or declarations of truth. And what is more, all things are full of perjury, broken promises, violence, wars, disasters and mutual destruction. But the worship of God either does not exist at all, or is lukewarm and insincere. Nor is pure religion to be seen anywhere, not encrusted with hypocrisy and Pharisaism. In a word, the whole world, even where it wishes to seem well-educated, erudite, polite, elegant and religious, is but a mask; except for the seven thousand who serve God in secret and pray to the Truth, and are known unto God (I Kings, XIX. 18).

3. If the scene of the world is to be changed, it is essential that all man's education should be changed, and that from the very foundations, in the way showed by Pansophy. That is to say, whatever men are taught and learn should be:

(i) Not piecemeal or partial, but whole and complete;

(ii) Not superficial and apparent, but real and solid;

(iii) Not bitter and forced, but mild and pleasant, and therefore durable. I shall show first how necessary are these three things (using the method already begun), then how possible, and finally how easy, if we undertake the matter with all our reason.

4. That all things should be taken as a whole and not piecemeal and partially, now this, now that, is shown by this very true thought, and the experience with which it is linked: that if the force of human nature is directed entirely towards one sole point, and not to the whole theatre of things, it cannot preserve a harmonious balance but oversteps the limits to a harmful degree, to the certain prejudice of itself, things, and other men. For if all the desires of man are not taken for fulfilment together, that they may be tempered, mutually complementing and connecting each other, then some will busy themselves only with things which can be known, others only with things which can be willed, and yet others only with things which can be performed; all the other things they will neglect and be disgusted by. Then when they are too full and swollen with this piecemeal business, they find on the one hand an over-abundance of superfluous things, and on the other hand a lack of necessary things. For example, those who long too dearly for power over others and do everything to gain it, oblivious of the rest; if they succeed in achieving their wish, they easily become tyrants, to the perdition of themselves and others. Others, turning only to pleasure, become swine of the herd of Epicurus. More noble natures prefer to admire the treasury of science; but if they exaggerate this habit, they become futile, unable to transfer their knowledge to practice and usefulness. And thus neither the former, nor the latter, nor the others achieve the goal of their desires. For those who long for power and empire, even if you give them the whole world or several worlds, will not be satisfied, as can be seen from the example of Alexander. Those who give themselves up to pleasure, corrupt their palate so that the more they drink, the more they thirst. Those who devote themselves to the accumulation of knowledge see no end to their studies, even if they were given the wisdom of Solomon, for the deeper a scholar penetrates into things, the more he sees there is still to know. 'For in much wisdom is much grief' and in collecting much other wealth is much envy, hatred and troubles. Yet mortal men do not desist, for they cannot wipe out their nature nor rid themselves of these desires turned towards things. If a remedy is

to be sought it can be none other than this universal one: that partial knowledge should be done away with and that we should all return to the complete simple and harmonious heritage which was to have been ours in Paradise, ceasing to divide the sciences, wealth and honours between ourselves, hurling them at each other and then snatching them back again, and thus conflicting. Let each man prefer to know, will and be able to do all that God grants us to know, will and be able to do, and not just some part of it. Then at last the happiness of every one of us will be complete, and not piecemeal, if it is not cut up, but whole.

5. But it is to be desired that all should be thoroughly educated, and not superficially, for truth, and not for opinion or appearances' sake, for the appearance without the reality is nothing but deception. Whither does this lead ? A dreamer thinks he has found treasure and become rich, or elevated to dignity he stands out above others, or sitting at a feast he enjoys his pleasure; but when he awakes he sees he is naked, scorned and hungry, and he feels the bitterness of ridicule; what good has it been to him ? And that such will be the fate of all those who did not store up true wealth on earth, when the resurrection of the dead comes, the Prophet has declared (Psalm 73, 20). And since Solomon declared that men who think much of themselves are lost ('Seest thou a man wise in his own conceit ? There is more hope of a fool than of him !' (Proverbs, XXVI. 12), and since the world is full of such conceited men, what wonder that all things are lost and the world full of fools ? If all men despise their neighbours and quarrel over their supposed wisdom, piety or eminence ? Against this evil we have no more suitable remedy than that all men should be invited and led by the hand to the true knowledge, taste, search for, finding of and possession of true and veritable wealth. Only then will it become possible to make all things quiet and veritable.

6. It is also to be desired that man should be educated slowly and calmly to spontaneous good behaviour and perseverance in pursuing the good, to real advantage. There are three reasons for this recommendation; first, just as at one time the philosophers used the externals of philosophy as a pretext for neglecting morals (wherefore they were called cynics, i.e., doglike and unclean), so it might happen that nowadays some people might use piety as the excuse for neglecting other adornments of the rational life; this cannot be allowed. For it is not right to leave the most cultivated of all the creatures in squalor of mind, word or deed; not even a gem will gleam until it has been polished. Another reason for demanding calm is that in such a noble undertaking (the true

reform of man and his surroundings) roughness and coercion might arouse disgust, while smoothness and calm (as far as possible) should arouse willing eagerness and even ardour. To this end, that once begun, this fuller education should not be relinquished, and that man should not be allowed to relapse into his accustomed torpor, inertia and uncultured state. For what profit is it to begin gardening, if you desert it again straight away and let the trees run wild? What good is it to polish and sharpen steel if you throw it aside and let it rust again? Whence it is sure that almost the whole of the human race, lying in squalor, is lost through its ignorant desires; for although nature has given all the love of truth, the good and the possible, there is no true, severe, constant education of their minds and nothing can be achieved by using those piecemeal, superficial and desultory tactics; all things sink back into their original chaos. Look at the schools! They are perpetually disputing, but they cannot convince each other that they should free themselves from noisy clamour and others from doubt. Look at religion! How many men attend God's school, the Church, their whole life long without rightly understanding even the fundamentals of religion. Look at government! For six thousand years men have been taking counsel on the best form of government, nay there have been disputes and even wars, overthrowing so many kingdoms, almost to the extinction of the whole human race. And have we with so much bloodshed at least achieved that which we were seeking? And do we not see that we must wish things to be otherwise, and make a new start, and strive that at last our longings may be fulfilled in all ways?

7. Someone may say: It is vain to long for the impossible; it is vain to attempt it; all things will return to their original chaos, as it has always been up to now. I would answer: To what purpose then do we receive so many complaints and wounds from God, and His exhortations which never cease? To what purpose are the constant impulses in us, and our longing for better things? Will God and Nature never achieve their ends? Soon we shall see another hope. Although we do not deny that there is difficulty facing such great desires, yet let no man talk of impossibility.

8. Let us concede that such complete education for man is not without difficulty, springing from four causes. In the first place, man is the most complex of the creatures, requiring for himself alone as much solicitous care as all the others put together, if he is to be preserved from corruption. This can be seen in the case of mechanical instruments; the more complex and delicate they are, the greater the danger of damage and

the greater difficulty there is in repairing them. Let clocks serve as an example; a sundial, once it has been correctly placed upon the wall, will last. A water clock, or a sand clock, which is a more complex mechanism depending on movement, is more easily broken and more difficult to repair. But even more so is an automatic clock; if it consists only of two or three wheels (to show the hours by means of a hand) it requires less care and trouble; if other wheels are added (for the clock to strike the hours) it requires twice the trouble; and three times as much if it is to strike the quarters; and very much more if it is to show the courses of the heavenly bodies or to play tunes. In short, the more parts there are to require care each for itself, the more readily the whole is subject to error in working. Such a creature is man, being of the nature of an element, a mineral, a vegetable, an animal and an angel; each of these parts again consisting of many smaller parts, and each of these again of smaller particles, every one of which is naturally apt to admit corruption from whatever source and spread it into the neighbouring parts.

9. Further, the constitution of human nature, by its very pre-eminence, is seen to be such that it will not be easily ruled. For man is not like wood or stone or the dumb beasts (which in their motions are directed only to one thing, or if to more, then only to certain things and along certain lines); but, like infinite being, he is a creature gifted with the ability to turn to an infinite number of things and to transform himself in an infinite number of ways, if occasion arises, so that there is nothing more changeful than man, nothing less capable of inclusion in fixed bounds.

10. The perplexities have been increased by the unfortunate fall of our first parents into sin, as a consequence of which we are all seized with a sort of dizziness, grow blind even to light itself, deaf to voices recalling us to better ways, suffering hallucinations even in palpable things, stumbling and falling even on level ground; the good we account bad, and the bad good; light we take for darkness and darkness for light; and thus we step on to the paths of death instead of the road to life. We are always more ready to follow ourselves rather than God, or those who stand in place of God, more ready to follow our senses than our reason, and those senses which are led astray by temptation and held captive, rather than those which are free. It is the inborn quality of all the descendants of Adam, a monstrosity handed down from one to another by the law of heredity. Although the wisdom of God, to restore us to a state of righteousness, became incarnate in human form and gave us an example of abnegation of our own will to follow the will of God, yet

He can but with difficulty persuade men to follow His example, even the tiniest but newly come into the world; for they, like the rest, have fallen to the level of the beasts and like them would rather follow their senses than be led by the reason of others. This is the reason why even the wisest err, the most pious sin, and many even with the best up-bringing degenerate. Although the spirit of Christ poured forth upon His church, given us by the grace of baptism, and invoked by the prayers and sighs of the pious, helps us in our infirmities (without which no man could mend his ways), yet this grace seeks not to remove but to reform nature. Our nature however saves its inborn character as long as it can, and thus begins that struggle between soul and body described in the Scriptures and experienced by every man reborn in God, in which now the soul prevails and the flesh is mortified, and now the flesh prevails and the soul is oppressed.

11. Another powerful obstacle comes in the way of bringing man to what is right: bad examples in morals and opinions, penetrating also (indeed, particularly) to young people, and bearing them off along the wrong path. Cicero himself observed this, in emphatic words which however explain it but piecemeal, for he was ignorant of the first man's fall and the corruption of human nature which followed it; his words must be understood in the Christian sense. He expressed himself thus: 'The seeds of virtue are native in our souls, and if they were allowed to grow, nature herself would bring us to a life of blessedness. But now, the moment we see the light and are taken charge of, we live in the midst of constant wickedness and the deepest perversion of opinions; we seem to suck error with our nurse's milk. Then when we are handed over to our parents and given into the hands of teachers, we are so imbued with various errors that truth gives way before vanity and nature herself before obstinate conviction.' Then when the common throng comes in as it were as the greatest teacher, and the whole multitude from every-where agreeing with vice, then we are wholly infected with depraved opinions and learn to desert nature herself. Behold, the multitude of sinners and evil-doers around us, inviting us to the same sin and evil-doing—this is the reason why the true and the good cannot always be implanted in young people with certainty of profit.

12. These causes of difficulty in education are true indeed, but at the same time it is equally true that if the causes are removed the difficulties can be either removed or lessened. Let us consider these things in order. Some believe that the best antidote for the multiplicity of human nature

(which causes it to turn to all creatures and be affected and infected by them) is simplicity, by which they mean that man should perceive the minimum with his senses and avoid profusion and variety in things. If we were to accept this opinion we should have to keep boys from the cognition of things. Let this be far from us! This is no legitimate remedy, nor does it offer what it ought. It is not legitimate, for it robs human nature (to which all things are subject) of its majesty and deprives it of its delights, and even tacitly implies some sort of blame to God Himself, the origin of the variety in things and the creator of the human mind. It does not offer what it ought, for a paucity of objects equally occupies the senses and leads the imagination to various trifles damaging to soul and body alike; all the more so, the less the senses are fed on the variety of objects, leaving the whole force of nature to concentrate on these few things. This can be clearly seen in country people and barbarous nations, for from the few conceptions they gain from their senses they form the most monstrous and pernicious opinions and habits, and are so tenacious of them that they would often rather die than defer to better opinions. If therefore you wished to make man tractable by this road, at all costs, then it would be safest to keep him far from all objects, or (which is the same) deprive him of his sense organs and make him blind, deaf and insensate (as we know some stupid fanatics have done to themselves at one time or another)—which means making a man a man no longer. But we are seeking the way to make man more perfect, not to destroy him. Thus it will be a sounder proposal, to leave the order the most wise God has instituted, i.e., to equip the most complex of all the creatures with all weapons to protect him from all dangers. For this Pansophy alone will be the natural answer, showing the right use of all things and preventing their abuse.

13. It would be equally sound to curb the licence of infinite liberty, by setting up barriers of reason everywhere in the way of the will, anxious to rush at everything; then it will clearly see that it cannot rush forward without coming to harm, and will curb itself. It will more readily accept the reins guided by another hand if it is already accustomed to curb itself in things which seem to it to be contrary to reason. Especially when all things can be so arranged that whatever man has to do he can do as it were of his own accord, without being forced, of his own will and pleasure.

14. No better remedy against the corruption of our nature can be conceived beneath the heavens than that which the Son of God shows us

right from childhood, when He was made man: the resolution to submit oneself to God, to do and suffer whatever is His will. 'Lo, I come' (He said as He entered this world) 'to do Thy will, O God' (Hebrews, x. 7). If man is to achieve this himself, he must be taught to believe and understand that our desires are utterly corrupt and cannot lead us anywhere but to destruction. Nothing safer can therefore be conceived than that man should elect God to lead him (for He is kindly disposed towards us as a father and knows a thousand times better than we what is good for us and what is bad), that he should pray to Him and leave Him to make all decisions for him; only thus will he not perish. This mystery of reasonable obedience cannot be explained to boys (and particularly young children) so that they may understand it; but it is possible to prepare the way to this understanding by carefully accustoming children to do the will of others rather than their own, that is to say, that they should in all things obey the commands of their parents, nurses and teachers. But let the greatest care be taken, that our commands and prohibitions be never frivolous, lest the boy (already beginning to use his reason) see in them something vain or unjust. For if this happens he will break the bounds of obedience and decide to follow his own will, either openly or secretly. Therefore since we are educating a reasonable creature, we must not deal with him otherwise than reasonably.

15. It is easy to find a remedy for so great a fault; would it were so easy to observe! It is for all opportunities and examples of scandalous behaviour to be ordered far from the eyes and ears of man, particularly in youth. For sins are not committed without imitation, nor can imitation be done without example; if there is no example to follow there will be no imitation. How to provide for them to disappear will be set out below in the proper place. For the present it is enough to show that nothing can stand in the way of our desires (restored to their original righteousness) to such an extent that we have to consider them impossible; we need only remove the obstacles, as far as possible.

16. For in human nature mind, will and the faculty of execution exist, fed on truth, goodness and unity, or unifying force, which is possibility. Human nature has such respect for truth that it believes even falsehood if it come in the form of truth; and holds goodness in such affection that it will desire even evil if it come in the form of goodness; and is so drawn to every possible good that it will attempt the impossible if it offer even a hint of possibility. (For men believe what is false only because they believe it to be true; they love evil only because they are

convinced it is good; and they attempt the impossible only because they hope it will be possible.) If then you offer the mind anything which is indeed true, it will seize it straightway; offer the will anything good, it will snatch it at once; offer the faculty anything possible and it will carry it out directly, if you make it easy too.

17. And since man has been given a mind of infinite capacity (with its parts, intellect, will and memory) like an abyss; and since this abyss cannot be filled either with little or with much; it needs infinite supplies of food. And thus unless the fullest light shines above this abyss the spirit of God (vigour of mind) will move above it, but the abyss will remain an abyss and will not take on the image of universal beauty. Let us therefore admit fully the triple light of God (all His works, examined by the senses; His lanterns in us, the dictates of reason; and divine revelation, accepted by faith). Then we shall see what the power of God can do!

18. Yet although our mind is of infinite capacity, it hates infinity (where no bounds can be seen to circumscribe and comprehend it). Therefore we can help it splendidly by offering it nothing infinite and vague, but only things limited precisely by the immovable bounds of their essence. Nor should everything be offered in all detail, but only the fundamental major parts; either the lesser parts will follow naturally, yielding themselves to the intellect, the will or the faculty like captives, or else they can be safely neglected until after the main points have been understood. All the more since the true happiness of man does not consist in great possessions but in the enjoyment of true wealth; so that he who possesses little, but true wealth, is less distracted and molested, enjoys more peace and leisure, because he has less fear of loss. Wherefore a merchant used to dealing in gold, jewels and silks finds it hard to come down to poorer goods, and similarly we, if we can lead men's minds to consider the greatest things in the world, will find it easier to lead them away from mundane occupations.

19. There are three conclusions which follow from the foregoing three chapters, i.e., that

(i) All men must be educated; therefore we shall need workshops for education, universal schools to educate all men; we shall use the term 'universal schools';

(ii) In all things; therefore we shall need tools for education, universal books which will contain everything; we shall use the term 'universal books';

(iii) In all ways; therefore we shall need universal teachers who will be able to adapt everything to all men in all ways; we shall use the term 'universal teachers'.

20. Up to now these three things have not been properly constituted, and the world has lain in squalor. For there are some nations without any schools, and therefore without any culture, only rough and barbarous ways; elsewhere there were schools, but bad ones, and therefore an evil culture, fit not to improve human nature, but to corrupt it more. Here and there were fairly good schools in scope, pious and holy; but not well arranged, labyrinths of hard labour. Wherefore we must see to it that they are set up everywhere, for the use of the whole human race; and that to carry out God's intentions, to renew the image of God in man, and not just patch it up; reducing all things to pleasant custom, they should become gardens of delight.

21. Similarly, some peoples have no books, while others have too many, not to help their minds, but to swamp them. Or else they are full of errors, philosophical, medical, political or religious. Or if they present the truth, because of the method they confuse the truth, so that they do not bring the profit they should. These tools for human education, then, our books, must be reformed in such a way that no nation may lack them, and their multitude may be reduced to number; by reducing superfluity to sufficiency, the free licence of thought to sound truth, and their troublous use to pleasant ways.

22. The same will apply to the teachers of the human race, that they may exist everywhere, being only good, and being both educated and educational, which means understanding themselves all things that make a man a man, and knowing how to teach them to others.

23. And from these things rightly constituted the following chapters will receive their laws: how to arrange schools, books and teachers for every age of man; and what they must be like; that is, pansophic, that all things may gradually move towards perfection.

24. This too will be a fine thing to observe and to arrange for:

(i) That whoever is born a man and brought to the use of reason should be school, book and teacher for himself; and in what way;

(ii) That every man should be school, book and teacher for his neighbour in their mutual conversation;

(iii) Finally, that collegiate schools, public books and teachers should never be lacking.

IESVS
NAZARENVS
CHRISTVS
FILIVS
DEI VIVI

Orientales
Hungari, Turcæ, Persæ,
Tartari, Indi, &c.

Aquilonares
Dani, Sveci, Poloni,
Moscovitæ, &c.

Meridionales
Græci, Croatæ,
Itali, Africani, &c.

Occidentales

Americani   Galli   Hollandi   Hispani

*Omnes gentes, quas fecisti Domine, venient & adorabunt
coram te. Pfal. 86. 9.*

Lux e Tenebris, A.D. 1665.

Chapter V

Universal Schools

The opening of schools in all places ; how necessary, possible, and easy this will be, if the matter is approached with reason.

Just as the whole world is a school for the whole of the human race, from the beginning of time until the very end, so the whole of his life is a school for every man, from the cradle to the grave. It is no longer enough to say with Seneca: 'No age is too late to begin learning'; we must say: 'Every age is destined for learning, nor is man given other goals in learning than in life itself.' Nay, not even death itself, or the world, brings man's life to an end. Everyone who is born a man must pass beyond all these things right into eternity, as if to a celestial university. Therefore all that precedes is the way, the preparation, the workshop, the lower school.

2. Wherefore both the whole time and all the tasks of life must be so arranged that we should be able to say of every man that he has completed his life before his life ends, and prepared himself for the life to come. For just as all things in the world are so ordained that through the wisdom of God each one of them attains its appointed end, preserving the order of things, so it is with our life, which is sufficient in all ways for all we were sent here to perform, if only we bear rightly in mind the purpose for which we were sent here, and use our means wisely, and make economic use of our lifetime so that none of it passes away in vain and the better is always preferred to the worse. Now for the most part we toss about aimlessly, and have more troubles in vain things than we could possibly have in serious matters, preserving the order of things; we swirl round in a perpetual whirlpool, missing the fruits of life. Men must be taught not to do this, but to go straight forward towards their goal.

3. The endeavour to achieve piety tends most in this direction; therefore all men should cultivate it, to have God merciful in life and in death; and prudence in life, to avoid all dangerous errors; and good behaviour, the universal spice of human conversation; and the arts and sciences,

essential for keeping up a decent life; and knowledge of letters, of reading and writing, for there may be cases where a man cannot speak but
through the blessing of letters, or cannot hear another but by reading
his writing. Since this may happen even among the lowest sort of men,
and since it is not so difficult to become literate that anybody may learn,
even those condemned to hard manual labour, and since even apart from
these unfortunate cases literacy has its daily use our whole life long, it
is quite essential to provide for all men to learn and know their letters.

4. Let all people of all nations learn all things; no impossibility and
no difficulty will be able to stand in their way if the bounds of the order
imposed on things by God are observed and its laws kept. For our wise
Creator distinguished His image (to which He could grant infinite
variety of semblance even if He could not grant it infinity itself) on the
one hand by different parts, the reason, the mind, the tongue, the hand,
etc.; and on the other hand by different degrees (which we call ages),
infancy, childhood, adolescence, youth, manhood, old age; if this is not
observed, then our time in life is lost, and with a double loss. First is the
loss of time; for what we could have learned in infancy or childhood,
we then have to learn in adolescence; and what we could have learned
in adolescence or youth, is put off until manhood or old age. And thus
either we shall not have time to carry out the last things we should do,
or else all things will have to be done in haste, that is, wrongly. The
second is the loss of opportunity and aptitude for doing a thing; for the
second age will not be suitable for that which suited the first, and much
less will the third be suitable. To give an example: a child can learn a
language (whichever you wish) easily; an adolescent or a youth with
more difficulty; a full-grown man with the greatest difficulty, if he can
learn it at all to a satisfactory degree; and so on. Therefore just as it is
the foundation of wisdom to manage one's time wisely, so wise management of the whole of our life's time will be the whole of wisdom.

5. It will be very easy, therefore, to make the whole of life a school.
Let each age be given only that which it is fitted to do, and the whole
life will have enough to learn and do, to profit from and pluck the fruits
of life from. For just as each part of the day and year has its lesser parts
and its proper tasks, so has our whole life: infancy and childhood can
be compared to morning and spring; adolescence and youth to noon-
tide and summer; manhood to afternoon and autumn; old age to evening and winter. And just as nature is always occupied about her business
in spring, summer, autumn and winter, never idle; so our life, if wisely or-

dained, can, will and rejoices to be busied at every stage and degree of age.

6. But the whole space of human life (given for the formation of body, mind and soul) is divided into seven ages: the first consists of conception and first forming in the mother's womb; the second, birth and subsequent infancy; the third, childhood; the fourth, adolescence; the fifth, youth; the sixth, manhood; the seventh, old age, followed by death. Similarly it will be most convenient to set up seven schools for the gradual perfection of man, namely:

(i) The school of birth, most like the beginning of the year and the month of January;

(ii) Of infancy, like February and March, putting forth buds;

(iii) Of childhood, like April, adorning the plants with flowers;

(iv) Of adolescence, like May, beginning to form all fruits;

(v) Of youth, like June, putting forth fruit and berries to ripen, and giving the first fruits;

(vi) Of manhood, which bears the image of July, August, September, October, November, gathering fruit of all kinds and preparing for the winter to come;

(vii) Of old age, which bears likeness to December, closing the circle of the year and consuming everything.

7. The first schools will have their place wherever men are born; the second in every home; the third in every village; the fourth in every town; the fifth in every kingdom or province; the sixth in the whole world; the seventh, wherever there are active men to be found. The first two schools could be called private, for they fall to the private care of the parents alone; the three intermediate schools could be called public, under the public care of the Church and the civic authorities; the last two could be called personal, for each will be so advanced in age as to be able, and indeed to be required, to be the maker of his own fortune, left to the care of God and himself alone.

8. We must deal with the public schools separately (for the time being in a preliminary manner). (1) What they are and why they should be erected everywhere; (2) that this is possible; (3) and can be done with such ease and pleasantness that instead of being troublesome places of hard work, they will be delightful playgrounds of the spirit.

9. I call the public schools assemblies, where the young people of the whole village, town or province will exercise themselves together in letters and skills and good behaviour and true piety, under the supervision of the most respected men (or women), in order to achieve a full

harvest of well-bred men everywhere. I will explain in more detail for this to be better understood.

10. I say the young people of the whole village, town or province, for it to be clearly understood that wherever a number of families live together, a common institution for the education of the young should be set up. There are sound reasons for this counsel: first of all, the parents alone cannot manage the whole task of educating their children rightly; indeed, many of them do not know how, for they are uneducated themselves; others do not wish to, by reason of their corrupt affections, the rich and delicate; others finally cannot, because they are too busy. If then nobody is to be neglected, common provision must be made by putting up public schools to which all men will have the right to send their children, and the possibility, and will indeed be invited to do so. In the second place, if a number of pupils learn together, it does not require so much work, but livens up teaching for both teachers and pupils, and achieves quicker and more permanent results through constant example and mutual emulation. Finally, the same reasons which moved God to ordain the gatherings of His church, and human wisdom civic gatherings, obtain here too, in as it were the prelude to church and government: i.e., that all should grow accustomed to sacred and profane converse, mutual concord, and rule their lives according to laws laid down for the common good. Let it therefore be agreed that public schools should be set up everywhere, as an economic advantage for the State, but as a foundation for the Church and civil government.

11. Further I say they should be committed to the care of the most respected men and matrons, meaning that such a grave matter cannot be left to any man of the crowd, but only to the most select; (2) nor to the young, who may not yet know how to rule themselves; but to persons of settled age and refined manners; (3) the sexes should be taught separately for the sake of decency. But to what end should all this be?

12. In the first place, for literacy; for absolutely all men should learn to read and write. I would add those skills necessary for life; for it cannot be allowed that young people should busy themselves in school with things they will have no use for in later life; but with things which will introduce them to the business of life itself. Let us here take as our own the fine words of Cicero dealing with the preliminary training of orators (*De Oratore,* lib. II), in which he warned that 'their training should not be like that of the Samnites, who before the battle shook spears which they did not use in the battle itself; but should be such that

the arguments they played with for training could be used in battle afterwards'. In the same way, I declare, young people in school should learn to handle such exercises as will serve them in serious work when they leave school.

13. It is in the public interest to remind people that young people should be publicly educated to good moral life. Just as there is nothing easier than for boys' morals to be corrupted by the crowd (in which individuals affect others by their mere converse, passing on evil either inherited at birth or acquired by bad education at home), so there is no more effective way of forming fine moral character than providing for constant examples of virtue shown in full sight of all, to kindle latent sparks of fire and grow by mutual emulation. In the first place, then, we must see to it that every public school becomes a public workshop of virtue, so that boys will not learn vice before they come to understand what it is—for it is hard to end what has become a habit. The habit of virtue should rather be contracted gradually, unnoticeably, so that when they leave school vice will displease them; as they write of the boy educated by Plato, who on returning home and hearing his father laughing loudly, expressed displeasure and said that 'nothing like that was to be seen at Plato's'. Even if at home (in the nursery school) the child should get used to some evil (through the inexperience or indifference of the parents), we must take great care to rid him of this habit publicly. For what would be the purpose of a bath, if it did not wash away dirt? And what would be the purpose of a school, if it did not rid the children of moral dirt, of vice?

14. Piety should also be publicly taught to young people, for it is the soul of all education and of our whole life; it is also teachable, i.e., it can be taught and learned by examples, precepts and imitation, the Holy Spirit aiding our faithful and humble efforts.

15. When I say that the young people should be exercised together, I mean two things: on the one hand that they should all come to school together and be loved and trained with the same care; and on the other hand that they should learn all things together. For in this collective way more knowledge can be imparted to their minds, better morals implanted in them, and more errors (with the passage of time) eliminated, and finally more work and money can be saved, if the best teachers are engaged not for each pupil separately, but for all together, to educate all of them at the same time in all that is necessary. In this way every public school will become: (1) a public school of health, where they will

learn to live in good health; (2) a public playground, where they will train agility and vigour that will be useful to them all their life long; (3) the home of light, where the minds of all will be illumined by the light of knowledge; (4) the home of oratory, where all will be taught the skilful use of language and words; (5) a workshop, where no one will be allowed to live in school (and later on in life) as the locusts in the fields, idling away their time in chirruping; but like ants in their nests, all hard at work all the time; (6) a workshop of virtue, in which all members of the school will be taught all refining virtues;(7) the image of civic life, where all will learn to be governed and to govern in their turn, as in some miniature State, thus learning from childhood to govern things, themselves and others (if fate should lay upon them the necessity of ruling others); (8) and finally the image of the Church, where from the appointed pastor of their souls and guardian of their consciences they will all learn both the knowledge of God and His worship; being catechized not only on the Lord's Day but every day, and imbued with various doctrines of religion by listening to sermons (appropriate to their tender age), exhortations and solace.

16. Finally I must mention the exercises; for in every public school everything must be alive with examples and practice, which is the short and efficient way of learning, rather than following the long and difficult way of rules. The words of Hoornbeck, who takes from Clenard the description of the method used by the Mohammedans to teach the Arabic tongue in their schools, are worthy of note: 'There is among them this custom—from their earliest years they are taught the Koran word for word by heart, impressing on their memories a book they do not understand. No copy of the book appears in any of their schools, but the teacher commits the text to memory and writes it on a wooden tablet, for the child to store away in his mind; the next day he writes them another text, until in the space of a year or two they have learned the whole of the Koran by heart. You will find many more who know the Koran in this way, than who have the book itself at home'. See how they hide their knowledge in their hearts, not in books, thanks to constant exercise.

17. Finally I would touch on the purpose of this recommendation to set up such public schools in all places, that there may be a full harvest of educated men everywhere. For if men grow up without education, they grow like the trees of the forest, like thorns, nettles and hawthorns; if they are to grow like plants and fruit-bearing trees they must be carefully planted, watered and grafted. Among those peoples where schools

are the rule, boys know, learn and understand more than old men else-where, wrote someone, I know not who. If this is so, then by setting up schools everywhere we must produce men who learn, know and under-stand, among all nations; then we shall have achieved what we are seeking.

18. There is no cause for anyone to object: 'We have had public schools, nor did we see such great profit from them.' We must consider the reasons why that has been so up to the present. (1) Schools as they are now receive pupils who are already spoiled by their previous educa-tion; if the evil things are to be untaught, and then better things taught them, it is double work, confused, difficult, and in many cases useless. (2) The pupils are not given into the school's care entirely, but only for certain hours; hence they return every day to their bad habits and get worse, feeling disgust at anything better. (3) In particular, hardly any ways were known of tempting the mind to better things; the major-ity of the teachers were more like to drive pupils away from themselves and from school, for their morosity and use of corporal punishment, or at least their sharp manner. But what we suggest is something very different. (1) To begin early with the right education will prevent the corruption of mind and morals; (2) kept in the company of wise, honour-able and industrious men, children will not be allowed to see, hear or do anything but what is wise, honourable and pious; (3) nothing will be forced or presented in a difficult way, but everything will be taught by pleasant, enjoyable exercises and games.

19. At this point some may and do ask, whether those of noble and of common birth are to mingle in these schools. I would answer: there are arguments for both sides. That the illustrious men of the future should not mix with the common people would seem to be supported by the example of David, who gave Solomon to Nathan to be brought up separately. Of course it is not certain that they had public schools of the type I suggest; it is more certain that they had not. And I put for-ward for consideration whether we could not begin the realization of that glorious prophecy, that the lion shall eat straw like the ox and the calf and the young lion lie down together? (Isaiah, XI. 6, 7.)

20. We would therefore recommend that public schools should be set up everywhere; for wherever men are born, education is needed that the gifts of nature may become reality, from potentiality. If only it were possible everywhere, someone may say; for perhaps there cannot every-where be found men suited for the education of others, or means for their maintenance, or other necessary things. I would answer: the essen-

tial requisites for a school are teachers, pupils, and good books; from the latter knowledge, morals and piety are instilled in the pupils by their teachers. Ministering requisites are buildings where people may come together; stipendia, for the maintenance of the teachers; and superiors who command authority and press for things to be done. None of these things can be lacking wherever men live according to accepted custom.

21. For wherever men are born in this world, there is no lack of pupils; for by our birth we are sent into life as into a school. Just as buildings can be set up wherever the materials for building can be found, stone, timber and clay; so wherever the material for schools can be found—young people—there they can be set up.

22. Wherever some men are outstanding among their fellows for their age, their knowledge and their skill, there can be no lack of teachers. For to teach others means nothing but to set an example in word and deed to those who are to learn. Thus the moment an example is given, a school already exists, and education can go forward; just as a building goes forward when a workman goes about his job properly with wood or mortar.

23. Wherever there is no lack of either teachers or pupils, there can be no lack of books either—the books of God. For all men have before them at all times and in all places the great book of creation; let them learn to read it! They have a smaller book within them, their mind, always opening to offer inborn truths, inborn desires, inborn impulse to action; let them pay attention to it! Even the third book of God, His divine revelation, can be available to all peoples; for either it has already been translated into the language of each nation, or can be. Nor need there be any lack of other good books, if there is no lack of industry.

24. Finally, wherever there is no lack of people who can hire a shepherd for their flocks, to support their family (be it a cowherd, a swineherd, or a shepherd, one or more), there can be no lack of people who can afford a keeper for the little flock of their children, one or more. The reason is, that more care should be given to the children of man than of beasts, and part of the profit from the latter should be transferred to the former, so that brute things serve rational beings, and the food for the body becomes food for the soul.

25. If anyone should still imagine some difficulty, we can say in all truth that in this way everything will be easier than it is at present, when only some are educated and the rest neglected. In the first place, it will be easier to maintain one teacher for all young people than (as we do now) many private teachers. (2) It will be easier for the teacher to teach

many pupils at once than each separately. (Ask an officer of the soldiery, whether he would rather exercise each recruit separately in the field, or all together; he will certainly choose the latter, and confirm that it is not only easier, but much more profitable.) (3) It is also easier for the pupils to learn everything together than when each is alone, because of the spirit of emulation. For the strong horse freed from the stable, says the poet, runs swiftly when he can overtake those he is following.

26. The matter can be made even easier if the place chosen for the school is one which young people can easily reach; in the centre of the towns, and if possible near the church, the shrine of religion; as far as possible, in a pleasant spot, green and shady with gardens or trees, and decorated with pictures; big enough for the whole number of pupils, for each class separately. As for time, they should either live together all the time, or at least be together for the whole day, so that going back and fore they should not be given the opportunity to do mischief or at any rate to waste their time and forget what they have been learning.

27. The way to facility in this matter will be a precise order in all things; for every school should be like a chain, each link joined to the next and creating a whole; or like a clock, each of the wheels so fitting into the next that when one moves they all move, regularly and harmoniously. So each school will have its set bounds, where it will begin and end; and within them divisions according to which work will proceed from the beginning to the end. At the same time it will be very useful to see to it that every public school and class arranges the sequence of its work like the seasons of the year. This means that the end and the beginning are most natural in winter, so that the beginning of the school year and the classes should be then, and not at any other time. In the first place, that all may be in harmony with all things; secondly, because people are less busy with public business at this time than at any other; thirdly, for the minds of all men (including the young) are more collected in winter than in spring, not to mention summer or autumn; for the contrast of the air itself makes the force of nature in each living body more concentrated. The feast of St. Gregory then, which is kept in many schools, should be transferred to winter.

28. The most important spice of pleasantness, however, will be the method of study, entirely practical, entirely pleasurable, and such as to make school a real game, i.e., a pleasant prelude to our whole life. This will be achieved if all the business of life is presented in childish form, not only for ease of understanding, but for pleasure too. That is to say,

it should be carried out with the aid of objects which cannot fail to give pleasure to children of that age, so that when they leave school and come to the real business of life they will think they are not seeing anything new, but only new and pleasant ways of applying them to serious things. To this end it will be good to arrange things in such a way that every school is as it were (1) a little economic unit, full of the exercise of the ordering of life; (2) a little State, divided into decuries like wards of citizens, each with its consuls, praetors, senate, and judiciary; all things filled with orderliness; (3) finally a little church, filled with the praise of God and devout exercises. In short, a little Paradise, full of delights, pleasant walks, sights and conversations; unprepared as they please, and then prepared for meditation; at other times questions to be made clear in answers, and letters to be written; finally, the acting of scenes, to achieve a good degree of eloquence. If this is done, then the praise 'a true school, pleasant work' will indeed be true.

29. Finally, in order to maintain all things properly as they are set up, it will be necessary to appoint in every school curators or wardens, called proctors, select men from the ranks of the magistrates, priests and citizens. They will keep all things in the proper order, for which they need not necessarily be learned, but very pious, serious and prudent; they must be such as to know how to regard every excess and return it to the bounds of order, they must wish to do so and have the power to do so, always acting with benevolent severity.

30. I add that all schools should have the reputation of being, and should indeed be, pansophic, drawing gradually on all things (1) sensual, (2) intellectual, and (3) spiritual (i.e., physics, metaphysics and hyperphysics); not separately, but all together through all the seven ages of man, starting from the fundamental and rudimentary, through broader and higher grades to the highest that can be reached on earth. This pansophic school will not be very difficult, but rather very easy, for it does not need laborious libraries, methods or teachers. A library will be (1) each man for himself; (2) all creatures around him; (3) the Bible, which every pansophic pupil must always have at hand. The teacher will be (1) each man for himself; (2) all God's creatures, viewed with reason; (3) within him the Spirit of God, teaching him, always to be devoutly invoked. The method will be always the same, simple and easy: always beginning with theory, proceeding with practice, and achieving chresis.

[Translated from the Czech by Mrs. Iris Urwin.]

The Panorthosia

Towards 1644, the world was a prey to disorder and devastation. Comenius hoped for a recovery which would be no mere return to a former state, but would mean fresh development and improvement. The result was the planning of the *General Consultation,* of which *The Panorthosia* is the keystone.

This 'Treatise on a Universal Improvement of Human Affairs', the sixth part of the *General Consultation,* shared the fate of *The Pampaedia,* except that a few chapters were printed during Comenius' lifetime and were available for criticism by certain specialists. The whole work may now be obtained in a Czech translation by J. Hendrich; the original Latin has not yet been published.

The Panorthosia may be compared with the *Via Lucis,* which Comenius wrote when he was in London in 1641 at the invitation of the English Parliament. The author had then shown that his plans for the reform of human knowledge and education could not be carried through without newly organized scientific collaboration on an international scale, involving the founding of a world academy and the adoption of a universal language to replace Latin, which had then begun to lose ground. These ideas eventually led to a plan for the general reform of human society. A new system of education, an international language, a universally accepted philosophy and a reformed religion were to be based upon institutions of world-wide competence: a College of Light (Collegium Lucis, at once a universal academy and an international Ministry of Education), an international court of justice, a world consistory, and an assembly where all nations would be represented.

The outline of the work is as follows: (1) plan for a universal reform, to be prepared by the Christian peoples; (2) an account of the causes of social evils and how they may be remedied; (3) an outline of the reform of 'human affairs', philosophy, politics, religion; (4) ways of carrying out the reform with the help of international institutions; (5) reform of the individual, the family, the schools, the churches and the State; (6) establishment of a 'universal council' (a kind of international parliament), the culminating point of the whole reform.

The passages quoted include point 4 (proposals regarding institutions which would carry out the reform) and part of point 5 (school reform).

Chapter XV

Once things have been so reformed that all things—philosophy, religion and polity—are indeed universal, the learned men will be able to collect and try the truth and impress it on the minds of men; men of religion will be able to draw souls from the things of the world to those of God; and men of politics will be able to preserve peace and quiet everywhere; as it were challenging each other to holy emulation, that each in his own sphere should promote the well-being of the human race as best he can.

2. The saying of Cicero is admirable: 'It is unworthy of the dignity of a wise man to believe what is false or to defend without hesitation anything accepted without due investigation.' Similarly let our theologians, who are to lead others to holiness, hold it incompatible with their honour to do or tolerate anything which is not holy; and our men of politics, the men of peace, hold it unworthy of their honour to give cause for dissension or to bear with it, not to speak of defending it.

3. In the meantime, however, since what is everybody's job is done by nobody, men outstanding among their fellows must be chosen to perform this special task; they will keep watch as from a high tower, not to allow anything unworthy of the reformed state of things (i.e., that nothing false, impious or troublesome should creep in).

4. If this is not done we cannot hope for anything firm and lasting; for the history of all ages tells us that even the best constituted things, if not preserved in good order, grow weak and loosen, in the end falling apart and slipping back into their old disorder.

5. Look at the Israelites, what ill counsel they followed, when after entering the Promised Land they gave themselves up to domestic employment, laying aside their arms and keeping no watch on the remnants of their enemies: the latter gathered their strength again, to the Israelites' distress. Warned by their example, and by thousands of others, let us

learn to fish with care! When we have so organized human society that the learned teach their learning, the men of religion raise men to God, and the rulers govern, let us give them custodians to aid them. Then it will not be so easy for indifference or torpor or sleepiness to return, for the enemy to find an opportunity to return while men sleep, and sow his tares.

6. Let the learned, I say, be given vigilant men who will rouse them to action to drive out any ignorance or error still hiding in man's mind. Let them be given to the men of religion, that with their help all atheism, epicurism and profanity still to be found may be driven out. Let the powerful be given custodians of their power, lest by abuse of emulation the seeds of discord should return; or if they return, that they should be weeded out in time and wisely, nor otherwise than to the private and the public weal of all.

7. Let us oppose the danger we fear (that universal matters concerning the order and well-being of the human race may become loose and fall apart) with a measure than which no more efficacious can be found: that perpetual custodians be appointed for the things once constituted piously; they will give their constant attention to see whether the schools are truly enlightening men's minds, whether the temples are truly moving men's hearts, and whether the body of governors truly protects the public peace; and will not allow aberrations either to creep in or to grow stronger again.

8. It is true that we shall have in every school, every church and every State custodians of law and order (I have in mind the proctors, presbyters and senators); but even so a constant gradation is necessary in all things, which should not be interrupted until it reaches the highest point in any particular sphere, and most of all where the eternal foundations of the common weal are to be strengthened. For just as people living together form a family, families together a community, communities together a province, provinces a State, and the whole community of States forms one commonwealth of the whole human race, so let each home have its tribunal, each community, each province, each State, and finally the whole world. Similarly the authorities placed over the schools and the churches to supervise their order and their progress must have their degrees, up to the highest point, where they are concentrated and where is to be found the power keeping all men and all things within the bounds of the common weal.

9. But there should be more than one such custodian of human wellbeing, as Christ, Wisdom Eternal, has taught us, in the famous words

of St. Matthew's Gospel (XXIII. 8, 9, 10) forbidding men to set up the rule
of one man, the leadership of one man, the wisdom of one man, among
themselves. He told them not to be called upon the earth

1. Rabbi		the learned
2. Father	which it is fitting to use for	ecclesiastics
3. Master		men of State.

That nothing should be instituted otherwise than that all men should
live as brethren, all with one Father who is in heaven, and who gave us
one Master and leader, Christ.

10. Therefore colleges will be set up in each of these three spheres,
the highest authority in each of which will be that Hermes Trismegistos
(God's greatest triple interpreter for man, supreme prophet, supreme
priest, supreme king) Christ, who alone rules by His ability to dispose of
all things with validity. In order to maintain order, then, some men everywhere will be placed above others, so that through all degrees of subordination Christ's school, Christ's temple and Christ's kingdom will be
firmly held together everywhere.

11. Would it not therefore be wise to set up three tribunals to which
all controversies which may perhaps arise among the learned, the men of
religion and the rulers should be referred? To prevent by their vigilant
care discord and schism among the first, second, or last of these? Otherwise we have no hope at all of bringing stability to what has been reformed.

12. It will be wise to distinguish them also by their names, the tribunal
of the learned to be called the College of Light, the tribunal of the churchmen the Consistory, the political tribunal the Dicastery.

13. It will be the task of the College of Light to ensure it will nowhere
among the peoples be necessary to teach anyone anything, much less
that anyone should be ignorant of anything essential, but that all men
should be taught by God. That is to say, to provide opportunity for the
eyes of all men throughout the world to turn towards that light in which
all may see the truth for themselves, and in which they will never again
be able to admit errors or hallucinations.

14. It will be the task of the oecumenical Consistory to ensure that
all the bells of the horses and all the pots, etc., should be 'Holiness unto
the Lord' (Zechariah, XIV. 20) and that 'there shall be no more utter
destruction, but Jerusalem shall be safely inhabited' (v. 11). That is to
say, that the whole land and the fullness thereof should be dedicated to

Christ; that there should be no scandal, no scandalous writings or carvings or pictures on any vases, etc., but rather let all things be full of holy emblems that every man, wherever he may turn, may find food for pious meditation.

15. Finally it will be the task of the Dicastery of Peace to see that no one nation rises against another, and that no man dare to stand up and teach men to fight or to make weapons, and that no swords or spears shall be left that have not been beaten into ploughshares and pruning hooks. (Isaiah, II. 4.)

16. Therefore let all colleges of learned men (such as the present Accademia dei Lincei in Italy, the Collège des Roses in France, the Fruchttragender in Germany, etc.) combine to form one College of Light, for the eternal Father of Light Himself calls them to unite in the community of light. For He said: 'Moreover the light of the moon shall be as the light of the sun, and the light of the sun shall be sevenfold, as the light of seven days, in the day that the Lord bindeth up the breach of his people, and healeth the stroke of their wound.' (Isaiah, XXX. 26.) 'And it shall come to pass, that at evening time it shall be light.' (Zechariah, XIV. 7.)

17. And let all the consistories or presbyteries of the Christian churches (such as those of the Greeks, the Romans, the Abyssinians, the Evangelicals, etc.) join in one universal church consistory, as is foreseen in the symbol of Jerusalem, 'builded as a city that is compact together, for there are set the thrones of judgement, the thrones of the house of David.' (Psalm 122. 3, 5.) Understand by this the Son of David, ruling His kingdom in such a way that there may be those who 'sit on thrones judging the twelve tribes of Israel' (Luke, XXII. 30), i.e., the whole church.

18. And let all the tribunals of the world become one tribunal of Christ, for when all the kingdoms of the world have been given Him (Psalm 72. 11, Daniel VII. 14, Apocalypse, XI. 15) 'a king shall reign in righteousness, and princes shall rule in judgement'. (Isaiah, XXXII. 1.)

19. Care must be taken to choose these select men from among the best, i.e., the wisest of the wise, the most pious of the men of religion, the most powerful of the powerful. Nor should the other desirable qualities be neglected, for wise men will be better guided by a wise man who is at the same time pious and powerful, than by one who is merely wise; the powerful by a powerful man who is also wise and pious, than by one who is powerful without either wisdom or piety.

20. Only then will the members of the College of Light in truth and in deed be what Seneca called philosophers: teachers of the human race;

and the members of the universal consistory will in truth and in deed be
what Christ called them: the light of the world and the salt of the earth;
and the universal rulers will in truth and in deed be what David called them:
the shields of the earth, or the defenders of God on earth. (Psalm 47. 9.)

21. Their highest virtue will be supreme concord and perpetual una-
nimity for the well-being of the human race; as if they were one heart, or
one soul of the world, made up of intellect, will and executive faculties.
Some philosophers have doubted up to now whether the world has a
soul; they will cease to doubt when they see that these ministers of light,
peace and zeal are as one mind and inspire one life and one salvation in
the world.

22. They will work together in concord to bring into the world light,
peace and happiness in the latter day; to raise the house of the Lord
above the summits of the mountains (so that all the peoples cannot but
see this light, and the peace and happiness which follow it); to tame the
monsters, like Samson and Hercules, should any appear; to stand like
cherubim with flaming swords at the gates of this Paradise (the reformed
church) and drive away all impurities; and like Noah to gather into the
ark of light, peace and salvation all living creatures to be saved from
destruction.

23. If anyone should ask how many of these progenitors of our common happiness there should be, it would seem best for every kingdom
or republic to have two, three, four or more custodians of the light for
itself, as many custodians of the peace and no fewer custodians of piety.
Let any of these colleges have one superior among them; and these
again one superior in Europe, one in Asia, one in Africa, etc. All these
together will be that Senate of the world, those teachers of the human
race, that light of the world, those shields of the earth, who will see to
it that philosophy is the home and bastion of truth throughout the world,
that religion is the home and bastion of piety, and that polity is the home
and bastion of peace and security throughout the world.

24. If I am asked about the place, and whether it is necessary that they
live together there—I do not think so. Leaving their bodies where they
will they can live together in the spirit, all doing the same things each in
his own place, and giving news each year of gains for the kingdom of
Christ, in light, peace and holiness. This applies particularly to scholars,
who are most closely concerned with this commerce of minds and
nations. Funds and means will be secured by the kings and states, with
the knowledge and good will of the churches.

25. It could also be arranged for the prominent members or their delegates to meet in a certain place every ten or fifty years, to hold a world convention where they would all render an account of all things and tell how the followers of light, peace and the grace of God have increased in numbers, and finally to give stability to this ministering rule of Christ; lest here or there a new Antichrist should arise, trying to become a new prophet, a new head of the church, or a new monarch.

26. But let us consider the tasks of these colleges singly in order to make this flower of human pre-eminence the foundation and the pillar of all order in the world.

Chapter XVI

The universal bond between scholars, the College of Light.

It will be their task to direct relations between mind and being, that is to say, to guide human omniscience that it may not exceed its bounds nor fall short, nor err from its path, in any of its degrees, conditions or cases; to extend the dominion of the human mind over things and promote the light of wisdom among all nations and minds, always for the higher and better. This College could also be called the Teacher of the human race, the Heaven of the Church and the Luminary of the world.

2. They will have to pay attention
(i) To themselves, as the ministers to the Light;
(ii) To the Light itself, to be refined and diffused by their works;
(iii) To the schools, as the workshops of light;
(iv) To the heads of the schools, as the light-bearers;
(v) To teaching methods, as the purifiers of light;

(vi) To books, as the vessels of light;

(vii) To the printers, as the makers of these vessels;

(viii) To the new language, as the finest vehicle of the new light;

(ix) To the other two colleges, as assistants in spreading light everywhere;

(x) To Christ Himself, the fount of light.

Let us consider each of these spheres of attention separately.

3. They will pay attention to themselves first and foremost, to be themselves what they should make others: enlightened, first and foremost, like the true luminary of the world; like the moon, I say, whose light shall be as the light of the sun, and like the sun, whose light shall be sevenfold, as the light of seven days (Isaiah, xxx. 26); like Solon and Solomon, the wisest of mortals, whose wisdom, maker of all things, taught them all such things as are either secret or manifest (Wisdom, vii. 21); like libraries endowed with a soul, living temples of the Muses, true torches of God lit for the good of the whole world. Otherwise, if through neglect and indifference these light-bearers become clouded stars and luminaries eclipsed, what will become of the rest of the body of human society? Christ did not pass it over in silence, saying: 'If therefore the light that is in thee be darkness, how great is that darkness!' (Matthew, vi. 23).

4. Then they will pay attention to the light of wisdom itself, which they are to make shine in beauty over all the variety of things and their universality, to clarify and purify, and to spread effectively over all nations to the ends of the earth. For just as the sun in the sky was not born and given to any one region alone, but rises for all men, turning towards the south and back towards the north and lighting up all things around; so the sun of the mind, wisdom, rising already now with such splendour, should not belong to one or even to a few peoples, but should follow its orbit over the whole human race; these apostles of the light will see and provide for this; thus will they be the brightest light-bearers, bringing the light of the dawn to the darkness of the peoples of the world, until such time as the sun of justice Himself, Christ, shall rise. And wherever that sun has already risen, they will take care that no darkness of the mind should return to darken the daylight of the Church, that no little star of partial knowledge already shining in the firmament of the Church should cease to shine, and even less that the sun of the Church itself, or the moon, should decline; for the Lord shall be its everlasting light, as has been promised (Isaiah, ix. 20).

5. In the third place they will pay earnest attention to the workshops of light, the schools, that schools should be opened among all nations and all communities of human society, and that having been opened they are maintained, and being maintained that they are lit with perpetual light. For just as the sun fills its planets with its light and shines over the whole globe of the world (except for what turns away and seeks shade among the opaque bodies); so the light-bearers will enlighten all the schools as the orbit assigned to them. They will therefore urge all the heads of the church and the civic bodies to tolerate no house, no village, no town, no province in which learning and wisdom are not taught. That is to say that there should be an elementary school in every village and for every so many inhabitants; a grammar school in every city; a university in every kingdom. And in order that everything may be done as it should be, teachers and tutors, curators and proctors should be permanently in attendance, and inspectors should come at certain times, preserving all things in good condition and reforming any errors which may have crept in.

6. Then they will have under their supervision the authorities in the schools, the teachers, masters, professors, rectors, curators and proctors; they must observe most attentively whether they all do all they should rightly, and endeavour to instruct those who are ignorant of their task, arouse the careless, and remove from office those who cannot be reformed; that nothing should be tolerated in these workshops of light but what is clear, ardent and pleasant.

7. In particular they will pay attention to the methods of teaching used by this, that or the other man in educating young people; whether they lead their charges to the fixed goal along the right road, over level ground, gently and pleasantly; or whether they still afflict them, dragging them by circuitous ways, along rough roads and over thorns. For even God Himself, taking pity on young people, has shown at last how all schools can be made into playgrounds; therefore we cannot suffer any school to continue to be like a grindstone or a house of torment for souls. Therefore that all schools should become gardens of delight, the members of the College of Light will pay the greatest attention to seeing that everything in school is achieved without coercive discipline, as far as possible, but not without it either, if the matter demands it; so that human nature is neither ruined by whipping Orbilioes nor weakened by indulgent and easy-going masters.

8. But a far broader field in which to employ their wisdom is opened to them by the care for books. It will be their task to see to it that:

(1) no people and no language should be without books any more; (2) that the books should be good; (3) that the editions should be unadulterated, large enough and easily accessible; (4) that books should not lie about neglected as they have been up to the present, but that everybody should read and understand them; (5) that they should be corrected and brought up to date according to the light that has been gained since; or that new books should be written, complete channels of the new light.

9. It will be their primary care, however, to see that as a symbol of the universal reign of Christ throughout the earth all nations should have His laws and ordinances printed, i.e., the Holy Bible: (1) in their own tongue; (2) in a correct version; (3) in a fair edition easily obtainable. For this is a greater matter than when Ahasuerus ordered his commands to be made known to all the peoples subject to his rule, in the language and the writing of each nation (Esther, VIII. 9). Aids from without are needed for the Spirit of God to inspire all men and speak to all men. The King of Spain issues his orders to his people in Spanish, the King of France in French, etc. Therefore let the Holy Spirit (Viceroy in the Church of Christ) speak to all peoples in all tongues, as He began at the beginning of the Gospel. Why should the mystery of salvation be taught only in the Latin tongue? It is not in this that the apostolic universal episcopy consists!

10. And since a foremost instrument in the reformation of the world are books, according to the words of the angel: 'When the world shall be finished, the books shall be opened before the firmament, and they shall see all together' (II Esdras, VI. 20); and since it is the printers that bring books into the world; this sphere also falls to the College of Light, to pay attention to them. They must consider what measures should be taken to avert dangers in the future, that in the days to come this art should be considered a sacred gift from God and one to be used only for the glory of God and the common benefit of the human race. This will be so if:

(i) Nobody is allowed to practise this craft without the permission of the authorities. It is certainly dangerous to entrust so great a matter to any chance person. For if the minting of money is reserved exclusively to the ruler and no private person is allowed to do it, although money is only the instrument for outward business; what measures should not be taken in such a matter as this, a thousand times more important and a thousand times more open to abuse? Nobody believes paper is made for anybody who likes to smear it as he will.

(ii) To this end let no man be a printer who is not appointed by the authorities and by the Church and by the College of Light, and let them be men of the greatest learning, wisdom, prudence and piety, and in addition let them be under oath, that the world may be protected from aberrations in this sphere in every possible way.

(iii) Nor can these workshops of light be allowed to exist clandestinely, or in any odd corner; but only there where those who profess the light live, in the universities, so that whatever issues forth, the very fact that it issues forth from this place should be sufficient testimony that it is a good thing; like public property accessible to the public, or like good gold or silver coins made in the public mint, it will be the public instrument for public trade in wisdom.

(iv) To make this matter even more secure and certain, let no one of the printers (however learned and pious a man, and under oath) publish anything according to his private judgement, relying on his own sagacity; but only what he is ordered to print by the public authorities, the king, princes, government, church, university, or the College of Light.

(v) Let no book be printed again, once it has been issued, without the knowledge of the same authorities; so that no opportunity of realizing anything to be added, deleted or emended should be neglected.

(vi) So much for the essentials. It will be an added advantage, and one which is worthy of an enlightened age, if great care is taken to see that in public books (and in future all books will be public) no printing errors are allowed to appear. Towards the end of the last century the famous Antwerp printer Plantinus enjoyed this fame, publishing books so accurately printed that it was considered amazing if there was a single error, even of a full stop, in any of his books. It is right for all printers to emulate this great diligence, for (1) it is a beautiful thing in itself, (2) it is useful to make the reader safe from error, even in the smallest things, and (3) it is possible, therefore, let it be done. It is certainly right that everything should be done as well as possible.

(vii) It will be easy to do this if (1) the texts are correct, clearly written, and read through again and again; (2) the typesetter is an educated young man with a thorough knowledge of spelling; (3) the same applies even more urgently to the proof-reader, who must be earnest and industrious, never letting himself doze. Or there may be two of them, the second of whom would receive a special premium for his vigilance, having sharper eyes. Plantinus himself took part in this work, looking through all proofs after the first correction, and then passing them on to the second proof-reader; if the latter still found any mistakes, Plantinus paid him a golden ducat for every one. Other incentives to diligence could also be used, such as the printing of the proof-reader's name at the end of the book, as we have seen them beginning to do in some books printed in Italy. Thus would the readers take care not to be nodding Homers, if they had to bear either public praise for their diligence or public disgrace for their negligence.

(viii) What I am about to say next may seem trivial, but it is part of the idea of the perfect reformation of things. If there should be nothing done without reason (and that without good reason), why do we see on the title pages of books and in the capital letters flowers, trees, little birds, serpents and what is worse, the most distorted monsters? Some writers and printers are coming to their senses, and not wishing to depart from the accepted practice in the design of letters, change it to something more rational; e.g., they draw Phaeton for the letter P, Elijah ascending into Heaven for the letter E, etc. The same is true of those who have started prefixing the titles of their books with pictures and symbols which foreshadow the theme of the whole book. This is a reasonable and beautiful practice, worthy of general imitation.

(ix) Finally the printers should be persuaded to leave the ranks of the craftsmen and associate with the learned, to carry out their divine task with a free and liberal mind.

11. Publishers must be requested and urged not to multiply pages, but wisdom; not taking as their goal the lucre of moneybags, but the enlightening of minds; that they may thus be true ministers of the light and not slaves of Pluto, creators of darkness and confusion. Let the members of the College of Light bear in mind that it is part of their supervision to see that this should not happen.

12. Since the finest vehicle of the new light is the new language, the members of the College of Light will consider it their duty to construct this language and spread it among the peoples, so that whatever new light on the new sciences, arts, crafts and inventions may arise in any corner of the world whatsoever, may become the common property of all peoples and nations; and relations between peoples all over the world not an instrument for visible profit, but primarily for the propagation of God's light among the peoples by the gift of the new language.

13. To this end they will be in friendly agreement with the other two tribunals, as with their helpers in the spreading the light over all things.

They will also support the other tribunals actively with their sound advice, like smiths and grinders sharpening their hoes, plough-shares and sickles, and resolve whatever knotty problems arise between the theologians and the politicians, so that the ecclesiastical tribunal will be left only decisions on matters of conscience, and the political tribunal only questions of violence and the remedies for violence. In future let the writing of books be a matter not for politicians or for churchmen, but for the members of the College of Light; for theory belongs to the latter, and practice to the former. Therefore whatever is needful in the sphere of theory should be sought by both churchmen and politicians from the College of Light. On the other hand, the latter will put nothing before the public without having had it tried in practice by both the others, and without their opinion and approval. Let the politicians wield the sceptre and give all their attention to the question of peace; let the theologians administer the Word, the keys and the sacraments, and give all their attention to keeping man's soul close to God. In this way their duties will not be confused.

14. The sum of all these things is that they should serve Christ, the light of the soul and of the peoples, that the nations should walk in His light—that at the evening time of the world the light may be clear, not like the twilight which went before (Zechariah, xvi), and that the earth may be filled with the light of knowledge, as the waters cover the sea.

Chapter XVII

The universal bond between States, the Dicastery of Peace

It will be their task to watch over human wisdom in governing themselves through all degrees and conditions, or even cases (which may happen) to maintain undisturbed human society with all its business, on all sides. In other words, to lead the propagation of justice and peace from nation to nation all over the world. It could be called the Director-ate of the powers of the world, the Senate of the earth, or the Areopagus of the world; the directors themselves could be best called the Eiren-archs of the kingdoms (the supreme arbiters of peace); Cicero called the Roman Senate *orbis terrae consilium,* but the name would be more appro-priate for this Dicastery of the world.

2. Going into greater detail, their tasks will be to pay strict attention to:

(i) Themselves, as the criterion and example of justice;

(ii) Justice itself, in all ranks of human society;

(iii) In particular the courts of justice and institutions of government, as the seat of justice;

(iv) Judges, as the priests of justice;

(v) The juridical procedure employed by this man or that;

(vi) The laws or the books setting out the law;

(vii) The interpreters of the laws, the commentators and notaries;

(viii) Measures, weights, coins, public ways, etc., as instruments of public equity and security;

(ix) The other two tribunals, as helpers in guarding order;

(x) Finally God Himself, the eternal defender of justice.

Each of these must be considered separately in turn.

3. Their first duty will be to be themselves first and foremost such as they are to teach others to be: just on all sides, peace-loving, pleasant, loyal; a true bond binding human society, true magnets drawing all men and all things to the pole of peace, living columns and supports of all order in the human race; Melchizedek come to life again, kings of justice; Solomon come to life again, kings of peace; Moses come to life again, diligent to reconcile fraternal disputes; the mildest of men, per-haps even the most heavily burdened with labours, and the strongest to suffer all things, altogether a lion's nature.

4. But it will not be enough for them to set an example of adamantine loyalty and to instil the love for it into all other men; they must pay attention to the way the counsels of peace are universally followed. Thus they will be the foremost defenders of the common weal, to prevent wars, tumults and bloodshed from returning, or the occasion for them; that all such things should rather be buried in eternal oblivion. Stand-ing thus on the look-out they will not stand watch only over the peace of one nation, or each only over his own, but over the peace of the whole

world, building eternal barriers to war everywhere, that before the world comes to an end the primaeval state of the world may return, peaceful in all ways, as Christ (Luke, XVII. 26, 27) and the Apostle (I Thessalonians, v. 3) prophesied.

5. In the third place they will turn their attention, to this end, to the public workshops for the preservation of peace, the courts of government, the tribunals of law, the assemblies; that these may be set up in every nation for the administration of justice, for the prevention of injustice, quarrels and conflicts, or for their early settlement should any arise anywhere; so that nobody may be left without refuge, defence and protection, if he suffers injury or fears it. To this end they will also pursue this special task: if any nation by God's blessing has so multiplied and is so hard-pressed by reason of its numbers that the native soil is not enough for all, it will be the task of the Eirenarchs to foresee this and take steps in time, so that the people do not seek their relief at the expense of others, as they have done up to now, unrestrainedly attacking their fellows or their neighbours, driving them out and killing them; but rather by founding colonies elsewhere so that all may live well, and thus fulfil the laws of charity and at the same time fill the earth with concord. This should not be done haphazardly and by force (as the Spaniards, Portuguese, French, English, Belgians and others did not long ago) but following the example of Abraham with Lot (Genesis, XIII. 8) using arbiters of peace.

6. The Eirenarchs will see to it that the public judges are such as the state of public peace requires, forming and strengthening them all to their own pattern (as has been said in paragraph 3). Let none of them tolerate anything irrational in the jurisdiction of his circuit, but teach and force all men to live together in humane fashion, and that rather by preventing than by punishing offences, troubles and damage done. For if anything should happen which could give occasion for discord, such as arguments over boundaries, etc., they will teach and admonish the people not to lower their human dignity by starting hatred and litigation for material things. For it is fitting for man to act according to reason, or if a matter of doubt arises, to try to judge, but not to act in passion or in anger, with force or arms; that is akin to the animals and cannot be tolerated any longer.

7. They will also consider by what means peace and tranquillity could be preserved throughout all human society without the use of violent measures, as far as possible; without prisons, swords, nooses, gallows,

etc., that the holy government of Christ's kingdom be not stained with executions; but if any man is determined to be obdurate in the extreme, it will be their task to seek and find means of subduing this indomitable malice so that it cannot cause public harm.

8. But to make it possible to be without this kind of extreme violence they will take steps to have written down all cases which cause trouble to human society, together with the remedies to be applied to each in good time; that it will no longer be so easy to disturb the peace in any nation, city or house. It has been thought that this has already been done, since laws and statutes have long been made and passed by states and municipalities; but it was but partial, more often serving custom than immutable standards of law, and never perhaps sufficient for all cases. Universal law must therefore be established, to serve the whole of the human race in all cases. It will be drawn only from the laws of nature and the laws of God, and will therefore be binding on all who partake of human nature and the divine light. They will also note laws which are doubtful, and offer general advice about them; and also laws which are obviously injurious and to be abolished for ever (Isaiah, LXVI. 2, 4). The Eirenarchs of the world, the supreme advocates of peace, will not cease to urge and press the scholars to write such books, immutable standards of law and justice, until that which is desired comes to pass indeed. They will also see to it that these laws are so well known to all men, like their own fingers, that no man can transgress under pretext of ignorance.

9. To this end they will have lesser inspectors of the law under them, and to them they will recommend these standards of law and justice, that they may direct all execution of the law according to them. And once a year, taking with them one or two serious men, they will visit all the courts of law and see for themselves how the law is carried out by this man or that; they will confirm those that work well, admonish those that err, and thus preserve the right course in all things.

10. These supreme heads of administration and peace will make particular efforts by their authority, favour and active support to help, support and maintain in vigour the other two tribunals; they will see to it that the authority of the ministers of the church, especially the members of the Consistory, is safe in every way and no less that the lights of the world, especially the members of the College of Light, can carry out their tasks of enlightening the world without impediment. Thus they will ensure the means of procuring good books and other essential

things, their distribution among the nations and their proper use; that
is to say, they will gain favour, urgency and the necessary money.

11. But the highest goal the Eirenarchs of the world will set themselves will be to defend the cause of the King of Kings, that beneath his
peaceful sceptre all the sceptres of the world may reign in peace, and that
all the crowns of the kingdoms of the world may be laid before the
throne of God and the Lamb. This will come to pass if every one of the
rulers is content with that portion of government which has fallen to his
lot by valid election or by heredity; let him not go beyond this nor
disturb the rule of others in their own sphere. The right to rule over all
things belongs to no man but the new Adam, Christ, to whom the Father
gave all rights over the whole world lost by the first Adam. If then any
man seek to rule over all things, he is seeking Babylon, bringing confusion into the world again. But he that builds the kingdom of Christ is
building Sion, the rule of the saints. And so these guardians of the
public weal will keep watch lest the kingdom of Antichrist, once destroyed, and the remnants of the wild beasts prowling the earth, should return again, and will put a curse on any who would try to build up again
the cursed city of Jericho (Jeremiah, XVI. 6). The Lord of Heaven and
earth will confirm the word of His servants, laying a curse upon the
house of Hiel, although he was of Bethel itself, i.e., of the very house of
God (I Kings, XVI. 34).

12. Thus at last will come fulfilment of so many prayers and supplica-
tions addressed to God the Father by the whole church for so many
ages: 'Thy kingdom come, Thy will be done, in earth as it is in Heaven';
fulfilment not of itself (for this is not the work of man) but by Him
who makes all things good, in His own time, and who carries out His
ordinary work in an ordinary way. Blessed are they who give themselves
to Him as a tool. Seeking the kingdom of God and His justice they will
find the kingdom of God; and under the reign of Christ (whom God the
Father has ordered to reign) they will reign with Him over all lands
(Apocalypse, v. 10), and this kingdom will be the kingdom of the saints
(Daniel, VII. 22, 27). Long live the King of Peace! Long live His kingdom in peace! from now and for ever more! Amen, Hallelujah! Amen,
Hallelujah! Amen, Hallelujah!

Chapter XVIII

*The universal bond of the Church, the members of
the universal consistory*

It will be their duty to see that the ties between the soul and God remain undisturbed for all degrees and conditions of men and in all cases; that is to say, to see that the reign of Christ is preserved in the Church and that the communion of the faithful throughout the world is maintained and continued without reproach by the subordination of all the members of the Church to a single head, Christ. The consistory could as well be called a universal presbytery, the synedrion of the world, the vigils of Sion, etc.

2. It will be their duty to pay attention to:

(i) Themselves, as those who lead others to piety;

(ii) Faith and piety themselves, that they may be ever more purified and infused throughout the church;

(iii) Churches and all sacred gatherings, as workshops of piety;

(iv) The heads of the church, as the guardians of piety;

(v) The art of planting the heavens and laying the foundations of the earth, and whether it is rightly used by all;

(vi) Sacred books, as the pillars of piety;

(vii) Those who write, distribute and use these books;

(viii) Acts of piety, the most glorious adornment of Christianity, particularly the virtue of charity;

(ix) The other two tribunals, as helpers in the Lord's work;

(x) Finally the Holy Ghost, the inner teacher of piety, the only source of true enlightenment, the comforter who protects us for eternity. Each of these must be considered in more detail.

3. Their primary task must be—since all who lead the Church in the name of Christ have been called 'the light of the world' and 'the salt of the earth'—to endeavour to become the leaders of the elect, the salt of salts and the light of lights; that is to say, to be pure and undefiled in all ways, holy and unblemished, true lambs and doves, the most pious of

men; so that if any iniquity be sought, there shall be none, and no sins shall be found (Jeremiah, L. 20); that each be a very David, a man after the Lord's heart; a very Moses and a very Paul, willing to lay down his life for his brothers.

4. In the second place, having been placed on such a high watch-tower, they will keep watch to see that everything throughout the Church is kept in its appointed place, that no injustice and from it no scandal may arise in any quarter; i.e., that no priest take his stand against his fellow priests and no Church against the other Churches for any differ-ences (if indeed any remain). And that no man, should he be shocked by anything his fellow has done, should scorn him and turn aside from him, nor that he should judge others and excommunicate them from the Church, giving opportunity for schism. For it would be unworthy in such a beautiful body of the Church as shall come to be, that the limbs should strive one with another; rather should the whole of Christendom strive to attain justification and sanctity, that the whole Church may be glorious, not having spot or wrinkle (Ephesians, v. 27).

5. In the third place, they will turn their attention to the workshops of religious worship, the churches; that they are built and attended in every nation and wherever people live together, and that they may overflow with the worship of God. Not as a revival of superstition such as the Apostle condemned (for the Lord dwelleth not in temples made with hands. Acts, XVII. 24), nor as if God could not be worshipped in spirit and in truth in any place whatsoever (John, IV. 23); but that there may be a place the faithful will be glad to enter, going into the house of the Lord to praise God's name (Psalm 122) and where the faithful will 'consider one another to provoke unto love and good works; not for-saking the assembling of themselves together, but exhorting one an-other' (Hebrews, X. 24, 25). This should not be neglected, even if nothing greater than a private cottage should be set aside for the purpose in a small village; in populated places there should be built enough churches to hold all the people, neither more nor less. There is no need of any magnificence in the architecture; only a fair appearance with no marks of worldliness.

6. Fourthly, they will pay attention to the pastors of the church and see whether they take enough care of their flock, vigilant to keep far from God's community all possible occasion for scandal and perdition. By this I mean pagan customs, feasting and drinking, fornication, the shameful Bacchanalian orgies and similar incitements to lust, and what-

soever remains of impurity from the world before the Flood, coming from Sodom, Egypt, or Babylon, and now destined to be cast into Hell. They will endeavour to free the streets of the holy city of Sion from all these leavens of the Devil and see to it that they are kept pure, not allowing any new impurities and godless habits to creep in without the knowledge of the whole world.

7. This aim will be achieved by allowing the whole garden of the Church to blossom with voluntary piety without coercion, that is to say without the key of priestly discipline, as far as possible; if this is not possible, then by means of the key. That is to say, they will keep watch lest abuse of the keys creep in, either through exaggeration or through insufficiency. This would happen if men in whom something of the insolence of Antichrist remains were allowed to rage against the people under the cover of spiritual power; or if indolent and lazy men, traitors and destroyers of the sceptre of the Messiah in His kingdom, allowed the power delivered to the Church in the keys of Heaven to grow weak, not using that power where they should (against 'every high thing that exalteth itself against the knowledge of God', II Corinthians, x.5).

8. If, even so, any man would desire to be a rebel against God's light and the enemy of his own and others' salvation, they must have ready those powerful weapons of God of which the Apostle spoke (II Corinthians, x. 4-7).

9. Once a year they will visit the churches under their charge, supervising, admonishing and encouraging, that every man may be content with his lot; or putting right any case where order has been disturbed or piety besmirched. They will be vigilant against any new heresy or simony, or that another Diotrephes may not arise somewhere.

10. If it should be found that there is a neighbouring people, or any men in their own midst, who have not yet come to Christ and His Church, they will most earnestly endeavour to bring them or to bring them back into the fold; that is to say, they will do all in their power to convert the unbelievers, to enlighten the faithful, and to sanctify the enlightened.

11. They will do all in their power to prevent what has been gained from being lost again, filled with ardent piety in all things. Therefore they consider it their duty to care for religious books and write new ones (with the help of the College of Light); by this I mean books which it is in the interests of the Church to have well written. These are particularly:

(i) The text of the Holy Scriptures (in the different national languages and in Latin, and then in the new universal language, if it exists); these texts must be in strict accordance with the originals, to the last letter. Up to now everything has been in confusion like that which reigned in Babylon, including these Divine works, as the Latin Vulgate shows, with its endless mistakes;

(ii) The two cherubim looking one to another, in the two ends of the mercy seat, that is to say the full, exact and uninterrupted parallelism of the mystery of salvation in Christ, revealed in both the Testaments. That it may be clear that what Augustine said, that the New Testament was hidden in the Old, and the Old revealed in the New, is not only partially, but completely true; for example, Micah, vi. 8, and Matthew, v. 7, 9, 45.

(iii) The three other commentaries to the Scriptures, interpreting them (1) through the Scriptures themselves; (2) by the light of reason; (3) by practical experience and select examples.

(iv) The most complete index to matters in the Holy Scriptures; using this advantageous method it would be possible to find easily any number of examples concerning any aspect of faith, piety or hope.

(v) A more precise index of words used in the Scriptures than we have had so far.

(vi) Celestial emanations as desired by Bacon.

(vii) General casuistical theology, which would solve all doubts or questions of conscience which arise or might arise, by drawing directly on the words and deeds of Christ (or even of the Prophets); to a considerable degree Erasmus gave a good example of this in his Theological Compendium.

12. They will give their earnest attention to see that no partial ecclesiastical rules come into being side by side with the secular, and against them, for this would offer opportunity for dissent and schism. If a church or an ecclesiastical teacher observes something useful, let him put it before the Consistory for their opinion, first the Consistory at home, national; and then, if it is a matter of greater difficulty, the World Consistory. If they see the thing is good, they will give their approval, and the matter will gain greater weight and usefulness than if it has only been tested by private opinion. The sum of this recommendation is this: apostolic approval should be treated as sacrosanct, that the spirits of the prophets are subject to the prophets (I Corinthians, xiv. 32); and no thought, opinion, habit or custom should be the private property

of any individual, but all things should be public and universal; that the garment of Christ (which is the outer and inner form of His church) be without seam, woven from the top throughout.

13. The members of the Consistory will see to it that these and other books useful to the Church of Christ are procured through the College of Light and distributed among the people; they will also consider how the books are to be used for the elevation of their souls, and whether this is being done. They will secure the necessary means for the writers and publishers of such books.

14. And since the poor are Christ's charge to us, the treasure of the Church, they will keep watch to see that the poor are properly taken care of. They will see to the establishment of almshouses and their proper up-keep, to cleanliness in hostelries and to the good morals of the people everywhere.

15. They offer their help to the other two tribunals, as helpers for God, thus increasing the authority of the latter by the authority of God's word entrusted to them, maintaining them constantly in this and praying for them together with all the people. That is to say, that all men should honour their teachers and schools, as the leaders and workshops of light, while they should humble themselves before the authorities, the officials and the judges as the visible presence and power of God himself. In order to achieve this more easily of others, in the first place the members of the Consistory must themselves submit themselves conscientiously to the authorities, while they will hold in reverence the ministers of the light, the representatives of learning and the schools, as their fellows in their calling, and so will bring them into the reverence of all men.

16. The sum of all is: they will consider it their duty to defend the cause of the bishop of souls, Christ, seeing to it that under His shep-herd's care all the flocks of the universal church enjoy their healthy pastures in peace.

They will take great care that nobody should introduce into the church new rites, or old but improper rites, which were neither introduced by Christ nor approved by the universal Church. This was not considered in earlier days (when under the rule of Constantine the Church was flooded with pagan ideas) and for this reason so many shameful practices took root in the Church. We must strive to prevent them from coming back as if home.

[Translated from the Czech by Iris Urwin.]

177

Short Bibliography

The bibliography given below includes only a few studies and makes no pretence of showing the real extent of the literature devoted to Comenius. Its purpose is to draw the reader's attention to a certain number of the works available to those who do not understand Czech. The reader should regard it simply as a guide; for a really thorough knowledge of Comenius' works, it would be necessary, in addition, several periodicals, e.g., Archiv pro bádání o životě a díle J. A. Komenského *(more recently entitled* Acta Comeniana*),* Monatshefte der Comenius-Gesellschaft, etc. *Among the publications of the past few years, the Czech-Latin editions of Státní Pedagogické Nakladatelství (State School Publications) of Prague deserve special mention. Up to the present time, they have included the following collections of texts:* Praeceptor gentium, Scholarum reformator pansophicus *and* Gentium salutis reparator. *For the three-hundredth anniversary of the publication of* Opera Didactica, *this great collection of pedagogic works is being reissued in facsimile, together with a Latin commentary prepared by the Czechoslovak Academy of Sciences.*

Works by Comenius

Korrespondence J. A. Komenského (Correspondence of J. A. C.). Ed. Patera, 1892; Ed. J. Kvačala, 1897, 1901; Analecta Comeniana, Jurjcv, 1907.

Opera didactica omnia. Prague, Editions of the Czechoslovak Academy of Sciences, 1957.

Veškeré spisy J. A. Komenského (Complete works of J. A. C.). Brno, Ústřední spolek jednot učitelských na Moravě, VIII volumes.

Die Grosse Didaktik. Übersetzt von J. Beeger und F. Zonbek. Pädagog. Bibliothek, Berlin, 1871.

Grosse Unterrichtslehre. Übersetzt, mit Anmerkungen und einer Lebensbeschrei-
bung des Comenius, von C. Th. Lion, Bibl. päd. Klassiker Bd. 10, Langensalza, 1875.

Grosse Lehrkunst. Aus dem Lateinischen übersetzt, bearbeitet und zu dessen
300-stem Geburtstage (28. März 1895) herausgegeben von Eugen Pappenheim.
Langensalza, Gressler, 1892. 8, 316 S. 3. Aufl. Langensalza, Gressler, 1902.
8, 316 S.

Didactica magna oder Grosse Unterrichtslehre. Für den Schulgebrauch und das
Privatstudium bearbeitet und mit einer Einleitung und erläuternden Anmer-
kungen versehen von Wilhelm Altemöller. Paderborn, Schöning, 1905.
Zweite verbesserte Auflage. Paderborn, Schöning, 1907. 8, 266, 9 S.

Grosse Unterrichtslehre mit einer Einleitung: J. Comenius, sein Leben und Wirken.
Einleitung, Übersetzung und Kommentar von Gustav Adolf Lindner. Sechste
Auflage. Wien und Leipzig, Pichler Witwe und Sohn, 1912. 89, 311 S.

Comenius' Grosse Didaktik in neuer Übersetzung, herausgegeben von Andreas
Flitner. Düsseldorf und München, Helmut Küpper vormals Georg Bondi,
1954.

The Great Didactic of J. A. Comenius, now for the first time Englished. With introduction etc. by M. W. Keatinge, B.A. London, Black, 1896, 468 p.

Didattica magna, tradotta da Vinzenzo Gualtieri. Sull'edizione critica del
Hultgren condotta sulla stampa originale di Amsterdam con introduzione di
Giuseppe Lombardo-Radice. Milano-Palermo-Napoli, Remo Sandron, 1911,
84, 412 p. 2ª edizione. Milano-Palermo-Roma-Napoli-Genova-Bologna-
Torino-Firenze, Remo Sandron, 1924, 23, 382 p.

Comenius, Didactica Magna. L'analisi dei principali passi. Introduzione e commento
di Mario Milana. Traduzione di Giuseppe Barone. Milano-Messina, Casa
editrice Giuseppe Principato, 1952.

Didactica magna. Version española por Saturnino López Peces. Madrid, Edi-
torial Reus, 1922, 321 p.

La Grande Didactique. Traité de l'Art universel d'enseigner tout à tous. Introduction
et traduction par J. B. Piobetta. Ouvrage publié avec le concours du Centre
National de la Recherche Scientifique. Paris, Presses Universitaires de France,
1952, 231 p.

Informatorium der Mutterschule von Amos Comenius. Bearbeitet von Jul. Beeger und Franz Zoubek. (Einzelausgabe.) Leipzig, Siegismund und Volkening, s.d., 66 S.

Mutterschule oder über fürsorgliche Erziehung der Jugend in den sechs ersten Lebensjahren. Aus dem Lateinischen übersetzt und bearbeitet von W. Altemöller. 4. Aufl. Paderborn, Schöning (1910), 6, 126 S.

Joh. Amos Comenius, Die Mutterschule. Herausgegeben von Dr. Karl Würzburger. Zürich, Zwingli-Verl., 1943.

School of infancy. An essay of the education of youth during the first six years. Edited with an introduction and notes by Will S. Monroe. (Portrait of Comenius by Hollar.) Boston, Heath Co., 1896, 16, 99 p.

Das Labyrinth der Welt und das Paradies des Herzens von Johann Amos Comenius. Aus dem Tschechischen übertragen von Zdenko Baudnik. Mit einer Handzeichnung. Jena, Diederich, 1908, II, 338 S.

The Labyrinth of the World and the Paradise of the Heart. Edited and Englished by the Count Lützow. London, Dent & Co., 1905, 306 p.

J. A. Comenius, The Labyrinth of the World and The Paradise of the Heart. Translated by Matthew Spinka. 1942.

Johan Amos Comenius, Orbis sensualium pictus. Herausgegeben von Joh. Kühnel. Leipzig, 1910, Druck u. Verlag v. Julius Klinkhardt.

Comenius' Orbis sensualium pictus. Anhang zur Übersetzung der Gr. Unterrichtslehre. Sechste verbesserte Auflage. Langensalza, Beyer, 1927. 10, 300 S.

Physicae ad lumen divinum reformatae synopsis... Cum versione germanica edita et notis illustrata a Jos. Reber. (Einleitung J. Reber.) Gissae-Giessen, Roth, 1896, 84, 551 S.

Ausgewählte Schriften. (Comenius Werke 2. Band.) Aus dem Lat. übersetzt und mit Einleitung und Anmerkungen versehen von Julius Beeger und J. Leutbecher. *(Informatorium der Mutterschule. Abriss der Volksschule. Die pansophischen Vorbereitungsschriften. Die pansoph. Schulschriften. Ausgang aus den scholast. Irrgärten. Welterweckung.)* Leipzig, Siegismund und Volkening, 1875, 16, 359 S.

Das einzig Notwendige. Unum necessarium von Johann Amos Comenius. Ein Laien-Brevier. Aus dem Lateinischen übertragen von Johannes Seeger. Jena und Leipzig, Diederichs, 1904, 207 S.

C O M E N I U S

Glückschmied oder die Kunst sich selbst zu raten. J. A. Comenii Faber Fortunae sive ars consulendi sibi ipsi. Aus dem Amsterdamer Druck vom Jahre 1661 mit einem einleitenden Berichte herausgegeben von Joseph Reber. Aschaffenburg, 1895, 67 S.

Zwei Abhandlungen des Johann Amos Comenius. I. *Über die Vertreibung derTrägheit aus den Schulen.* II. *Aus den Schul-Labyrinthen Ausgang ins Freie.* Übersetzt von C. Th. Lion. (Vorbemerkungen.) Hannover-Linden, Manz und Lange, 1894, 55 S.

Johann Amos Comenius. Ausgewählte Schriften zur Reform in Wissenschaft, Religion u. Politik... Übersetzt und bearbeitet von Herbert Schönebaum. Leipzig, Kröner, 1924.

J. A. Comenius, Schola Ludus, d.i. die Schule als Spiel oder lebendige Encyklopädie, d. h. die 'Sprachenpforte'. Dramatische Darstellung ins Deutsche übertragen von Wilhelm Bötticher. Langensalza, Beyer, 1886. XV, 373 S.

J. A. Comenius, Two Pansophical Works. I. *Praecognita.* II. *Janua Rerum 1643.* Edited by G. H. Turnbull, Praha, Česka akademie věd a uměni, 1951, 171 p.

Works concerning Comenius

BEISSWÄNGER, Gustav. *Amos Comenius als Pansoph. Eine historisch-philosophische Untersuchung.* Stuttgart, 1904.

BOVET, P. *Jean Amos Comenius, Un patriote cosmopolite.* Genève, Rosello, 1943.

BUISSON, F. *Nouveau dictionnaire de pédagogie et d'instruction primaire.* Paris, 1911, article Comenius, p. 325-9.

CRIEGERN, Hermann Ferdinand von. *Johann Amos Comenius als Theolog.* Leipzig, Heidelberg, 1881.

CYZEVSKIJ, Dimitrij. 'Comeniana', *Zeitschrift für slavische Philologie,* XII, 1935, 179 ff.; XIX, 1947, 410 ff.; XX, 1950, 144 ff.

—. *Analecta Comeniana.* Kyrios II, 1937.

—. *Comenius' Labyrinth of world, its themes and sources.* Harvard, Slavic Studies, 1953.

181

CYZEVSKIJ, Dimitrij. 'Das Labyrinth der Welt und das Paradies des Herzens des J. A. Comenius', *Wiener Slavistisches Jahrbuch* V, 1957.

DENIS, Ernest. *La Bohême depuis la Montagne blanche.* Paris, 1903, p. 219-33.

DILTHEY, Wilhelm. *Pädagogik.* Leipzig, Teubner, 1934, p. 160-5.

GINDELY, A. *Über des J. A. Comenius Leben und Wirksamkeit in der Fremde.* Heft 6, Znaim, 1892.

HENDRICH, Jos. *Jan Amos Komensky (Comenius).* Translated from the Czech by Bohdan Goldreich. Prague, Orbis, 1948.

HERDER, J. G. *Johann Amos Comenius* . . . Herausgegeben von Koller. Berlin, Unger, 1903.

—. *Briefe zur Beförderung der Humanität (Comenius, Ein Charakterbild . . .)* Riga, 1795 ; Berlin, 1903.

HEYBERGER, Anna. *Jean Amos Comenius (Komensky). Sa vie et son œuvre d'éduca-teur.* Paris, Honoré Champion, 1928.

HUTTON, J. E. *A history of the Moravian church.* London, 1909.

JAKUBEK, Jan. *J. A. Comenius.* Praha, Čes. akad. věd a uměni, 1928. (English text.)

KVAČALA, J. *J. A. Comenius.* Berlin 1914. Lehmann series: *Die grossen Erzieher. Ihre Persönlichkeit und ihre Systeme.*

—. *Die pädagogische Reform des Comenius in Deutschland bis zum Ausgange des XVII. Jahrhunderts.* Two volumes, Berlin, 1903 and 1904, in the *Monumenta Germaniae paedagogica.*

—. 'Die letzten autobiographischen Aufzeichnungen des Comenius', *Zeitschrift für Geschichte der Erziehung u. Unterrichts.* Jahrgang 3, 1913.

LAURIE, S. S. *Johann Amos Comenius, Bishop of the Moravians, his life and educational works.* London, 1899.

MICHELET, J. *Nos fils.* Paris, 1869, livre III, p. 175-8.

MONROE, Will S. *Comenius, the evangelist of modern pedagogy.* Boston, 1892.

ORESTANO, Francesco. *Comenio.* Roma, 1906, 131 p.

QUICK, Robert Hebert. *Essays on educational reformers.* New York, Appleton & Co., 1868. Chap. X: 'Comenius'.

ROBERT, Edouard. 'Notice sur Jean Amos Comenius et ses idées humanitaires et pédagogiques. Travail lu le 15 avril 1881, à Alger, devant la 16e section de l'Association française pour l'avancement des sciences', extrait de *La Revue pédagogique,* décembre 1881, février 1882.

SPRANGER, E. 'Comenius, ein Mann der Sehnsucht', in: *Kultur und Erziehung.* Leipzig, Quelle u. Meyer, 1922 et seq.

TURNBULL, G. H. *Samuel Hartlib. A sketch of his life and his relations to J. A. Comenius.* Oxford University Press, 1920.

—. *Hartlib, Dury and Comenius.* Liverpool, 1947.

YOUNG, Rob. Fitzg. *Comenius in England* 1641/2. London, Oxford University Press, 1932.